SPORTS ENCYCLOPEDIAS FOR KIDS

THE NBA
ENCYCLOPEDIA FOR KIDS

BY BRENDAN FLYNN

Abdo Reference

An Imprint of Abdo Publishing
abdobooks.com

D1518821

TABLE OF CONTENTS

THE HISTORY OF THE
NATIONAL BASKETBALL ASSOCIATION

The history of professional basketball in the United States dates to the late 1800s, shortly after the game was invented. But the history of the National Basketball Association (NBA) begins in 1937. That's when the National Basketball League (NBL) was formed. The NBL began with 13 teams. Most of them were in the Midwest. Some cities struggled to keep teams.

More than seven decades after the NBA's founding, the league continues to thrive.

More than 35 teams played at least one season in the NBL during its 12-year run.

Meanwhile in Boston, Massachusetts, Walter Brown noticed fans' appetite for the game. Brown owned the Boston Garden. This was a famous arena in the city's downtown area. He saw how the NBL had found a way to stay in business despite its struggles. He thought it was time to bring professional basketball to bigger cities.

Brown gathered businesspeople from around the country. They created the Basketball Association of America (BAA). The BAA began with 11 clubs in 1946. The teams played in modern arenas like the Boston Garden and Madison Square Garden in New York.

Basketball began with James Naismith, who invented the sport in 1891.

Madison Square Garden is one of the most famous sports venues in the world.

Just like the NBL, though, many BAA teams had trouble establishing themselves in their cities. Only eight teams suited up for the league's second season. League owners chose Maurice Podoloff as the BAA's first commissioner. Podoloff soon realized that the BAA lacked the one thing it needed the most: a star player.

MIGHTY MIKAN

George Mikan was basketball's first true superstar. The 6-foot-10 center towered over opponents while playing at DePaul University in Chicago, Illinois. Wearing his famous No. 99 jersey and glasses that made him look more like a teacher than one of the world's top athletes, Mikan was nearly unstoppable. Fans flocked to watch him block shots at one end

HARLEM GLOBETROTTERS

One of the most important people in the early days of professional basketball never played an actual game. Abe Saperstein was a 24-year-old businessperson. He started promoting a team of players he called the Savoy Big Five in 1926. The team got its name from the Savoy Ballroom, a music and sports venue in Chicago. Saperstein kept changing the name of his team in the early days, eventually settling on the Harlem Globetrotters.

The Globetrotters really did trot all over the globe, winning wherever they went. Sometimes the Globetrotters would be winning by so much, they'd start goofing off late in games. The crowd ate it up, and soon their on-court antics became a regular part of each contest. The Globetrotters became ambassadors for the game all over the world, a tradition that continues to this day. The Globetrotters have played in more than 120 countries and territories all over the world.

George Mikan's height helped him dominate professional basketball in the late 1940s and early 1950s.

of the court and drop in basket after basket at the other with his famous hook shot.

After graduating from DePaul, Mikan decided to stay in Chicago. He played for the NBL's Chicago American Gears. He helped the Gears to the NBL title as a rookie. Mikan joined the Minneapolis Lakers the following season. He was even better there. Mikan led the league with 21.3 points per game. He guided the Lakers to the championship.

Podoloff understood that for the BAA to survive, it needed Mikan. Podoloff approached the owners of the Lakers and three other NBL teams in 1948. He talked them into joining the BAA.

Mikan dominated the middle as the Lakers steamrolled their way to the BAA title in their first season in the league. With Mikan now in the BAA, the NBL had trouble staying in business. Before the 1949–50 season, the remaining teams decided to join the BAA. But the combined 17-team league needed a new name. On August 3, 1949, the NBA was born.

CHALLENGES AND SUCCESSES

The new league faced challenges in its early years. But the NBA had Mikan to help lead the way. The Lakers were the NBA's first dynasty. With Mikan patrolling the lane, Minneapolis won five NBA championships between 1949 and 1954. Mikan was

THE NEW YORK RENS BREAK BARRIERS

The New York Renaissance, also known as the Rens, was the first all-Black pro team. Founded in the Harlem neighborhood of New York City in the 1920s, the Rens played a fast-paced style that dared their opponents to keep up. Most of them couldn't. The Rens were one of basketball's first super teams. They won 88 straight games in the span of 86 days in 1932–33. In 1939, they captured the first World Professional Tournament Championship. The Rens wanted to play in a professional league, but none of the leagues at the time allowed Black players. The Rens were forced to go on tours from city to city to take on local teams. They helped prove basketball players could be great regardless of skin color. The Rens won more than 2,000 games before disbanding in 1949.

so good that the new league was forced to change its rules to make it fairer for other teams.

The NBA widened the lane from 6 feet (1.8 m) to 12 feet (3.7 m). That way, Mikan couldn't just stand next to the basket,

In today's NBA, the shot clock is located directly above each basket, below the game clock.

blocking shots at one end and making easy baskets at the other. The league made other changes in this era too. It adopted a 24-second shot clock so teams would be forced to shoot. That helped increase the pace of play. This led to the high-intensity action the NBA is known for today.

THE CELTICS' DYNASTY

The NBA's next power team emerged in Boston. Celtics coach Arnold "Red" Auerbach had an eye for talent, and he wasn't afraid to make bold decisions. Shortly after taking over in Boston, he worked to make guard Chuck Cooper the first Black player to be drafted into the NBA. The Celtics selected Cooper in the second round of the 1950 draft. The decision opened the NBA's doors to non-white players. It sent the message that the league was open to the best players in the world, regardless of race.

Auerbach was just getting started. In 1956, he made a trade with the St. Louis Hawks to get the second pick in the draft. This gave him the chance to get Bill Russell. The 6-foot-10 Russell turned Boston into a powerhouse. The Celtics didn't simply win after Russell hopped on board. They dominated. Boston won the championship 11 times during a 13-year stretch starting in 1957. That included eight consecutive titles

Arnold "Red" Auerbach, *right*, coached many legendary stars in his career, including Bob Cousy.

from 1959 through 1966. No franchise before or since has come close to challenging the Celtics' dynasty.

Russell himself made history when Auerbach stepped down from coaching in 1966. Russell took over as a player-coach.

Bill Russell (6) was a force to be reckoned with on the court.

That made the game-changing center the first Black head coach in NBA history. Russell guided the Celtics to two more NBA titles. The team grabbed one in 1968 and another in 1969.

Russell (6) and Auerbach were key figures in the Boston Celtics' dynasty.

A NEW RIVAL

Starting in the late 1960s, the NBA had to compete with a rival league, the American Basketball Association (ABA). The ABA paid big money to college stars. Some of the greatest players of all time began their careers there, while others left the NBA for the new league. Forward Rick Barry left the NBA's San Francisco Warriors to join the ABA's Oakland Oaks. Artis Gilmore powered the ABA's Kentucky Colonels.

THE ABA

To help attract fans, the ABA tried many ideas, some of which are still common in today's NBA. The ABA gave the sport the three-point line and the first professional Slam Dunk Contest. The league was also known for its red, white, and blue ball. Still, the upstart league was rarely on national television and didn't receive much national media attention. The ABA joined the NBA in 1976. The following year, ten of the NBA's 24 All-Stars were former ABA players.

No player in the upstart league soared higher than Julius Erving. He was known for his jaw-dropping dunks for the Virginia Squires and New York Nets. His stunning moves gave the basketball world a jolt. Before Erving came along, the dunk was just the easiest way to score two points. Erving turned dunking into an art form. In the first Slam Dunk Contest, held before the 1976 ABA All-Star Game, Erving ran the length of the court, took off at the foul line 15 feet (4.6 m) from the basket, and appeared to fly toward the hoop before jamming the ball through the net. The crowd roared in approval.

Though the ABA merged with the NBA in 1976, the upstart league's legacy lives on. Erving's arrival in 1976 put the NBA on track to reach the same popularity as the National Football

Julius Erving's high-flying dunks wowed fans in the ABA before he joined the NBA for the last decade of his career.

League and Major League Baseball. Erving could do a lot of things with a basketball. His hands were so large he could grab a ball and squeeze it like an orange. He could thunder down the lane for a dunk. He could also swoop under the basket for a graceful layup. In many ways, Erving was the NBA's first made-for-TV superstar. He had the good looks, the smile, and most importantly, the skills to bring fans to the arena. The one thing Erving couldn't do was take the NBA to the next level by himself, no matter how great a player he was. He needed help. And in the winter of 1979, it arrived.

MAGIC, BIRD, AND JORDAN

In 1979, two stunning rookies came to the NBA. Earvin "Magic" Johnson was a star point guard at Michigan State. His Spartans won the college basketball national title. They defeated Larry Bird's Indiana State team in the championship game. Johnson and Bird transformed the NBA when they joined the league. Bird breathed new life into the Celtics. Johnson led the Los Angeles Lakers to the NBA title in his first year.

Bird's Celtics and Johnson's Lakers battled for NBA supremacy throughout the 1980s. But the 1990s belonged to one man and one team: Michael Jordan and the Chicago Bulls.

BUSINESS PARTNERS

Companies lined up to cash in on the success of Bird and Johnson. The two often did endorsement deals together. Shoe company Converse signed both of them, giving each a signature shoe in their respective team's colors. In 1986, the two met in French Lick, Indiana, to shoot a commercial. They put aside their rivalry to begin a lifelong friendship.

Larry Bird (33) and Magic Johnson (32) became the faces of the NBA in the 1980s.

The intense guard took the NBA by storm as a rookie in 1984–85. He averaged 28.2 points per game. He also earned the nickname "Air Jordan" for his soaring dunks. He was named NBA's Rookie of the Year and signed an endorsement contract with Nike.

It took a while for the Bulls to assemble enough talent around Jordan to build a championship team. But with head coach Phil Jackson and forward Scottie Pippen on board, the Bulls were the NBA's top team of the 1990s. They won three straight league titles starting in 1991. Then, beginning in 1996 after Jordan's return from retirement, they won three in a row again.

Jackson moved on to coach in Los Angeles. He teamed with center Shaquille O'Neal and guard Kobe Bryant to win three straight titles starting in the 1999–2000 season. After O'Neal

Michael Jordan soars for a layup during a 1991 game.

left, the Lakers won two more championships in 2009 and 2010. This gave Jackson a record 11 titles as a head coach.

The San Antonio Spurs challenged the Lakers for NBA supremacy during that time. Head coach Gregg Popovich led the Spurs to five titles between 1999 and 2014. Center David Robinson, forward Tim Duncan, and point guard Tony Parker were the mainstays during that run.

KING JAMES

The next face of the NBA wore Jordan's familiar No. 23 jersey. LeBron James drew comparisons to everyone from Jordan to Magic Johnson. The spotlight found James while

Lakers center Shaquille O'Neal, *left*, hugs Kobe Bryant after a 2001 game.

he was still playing for St. Vincent–St. Mary High in Akron, Ohio. *Sports Illustrated* magazine put James on its cover in February 2002, when James was a high school junior. The headline read "The Chosen One."

LeBron James arrived in the NBA with huge expectations.

James came along at just the right time for the Cleveland Cavaliers. The team won the draft lottery in 2003. Everyone knew they would select 18-year-old James. James gave the Cavaliers and the NBA a fresh face to build around.

James made the Cavs competitive, but they couldn't get over the top. To win an NBA title, James decided he needed to leave his hometown and head south. He joined the Miami Heat in 2010. With guard Dwyane Wade and forward Chris

James (6), Dwyane Wade (3), and Chris Bosh (1) took part in a ceremony to welcome James and Bosh to Miami in July 2010.

Stephen Curry, *left*, is one of the most recognizable players in the NBA today.

Bosh, James helped the team win the league championship twice in the next four years.

Meanwhile, another dynasty was emerging on the West Coast. Behind the deadly shooting touch of guard Stephen Curry, the Golden State Warriors became the hottest team in the league. Curry and teammate Klay Thompson rained down three-pointers from all over the court, while forward Draymond Green cleaned up any misses. The Warriors won the NBA title in 2015. With former most valuable player (MVP) forward Kevin Durant added to the mix, they won again in 2017 and 2018. They fell short only when James returned to Cleveland and

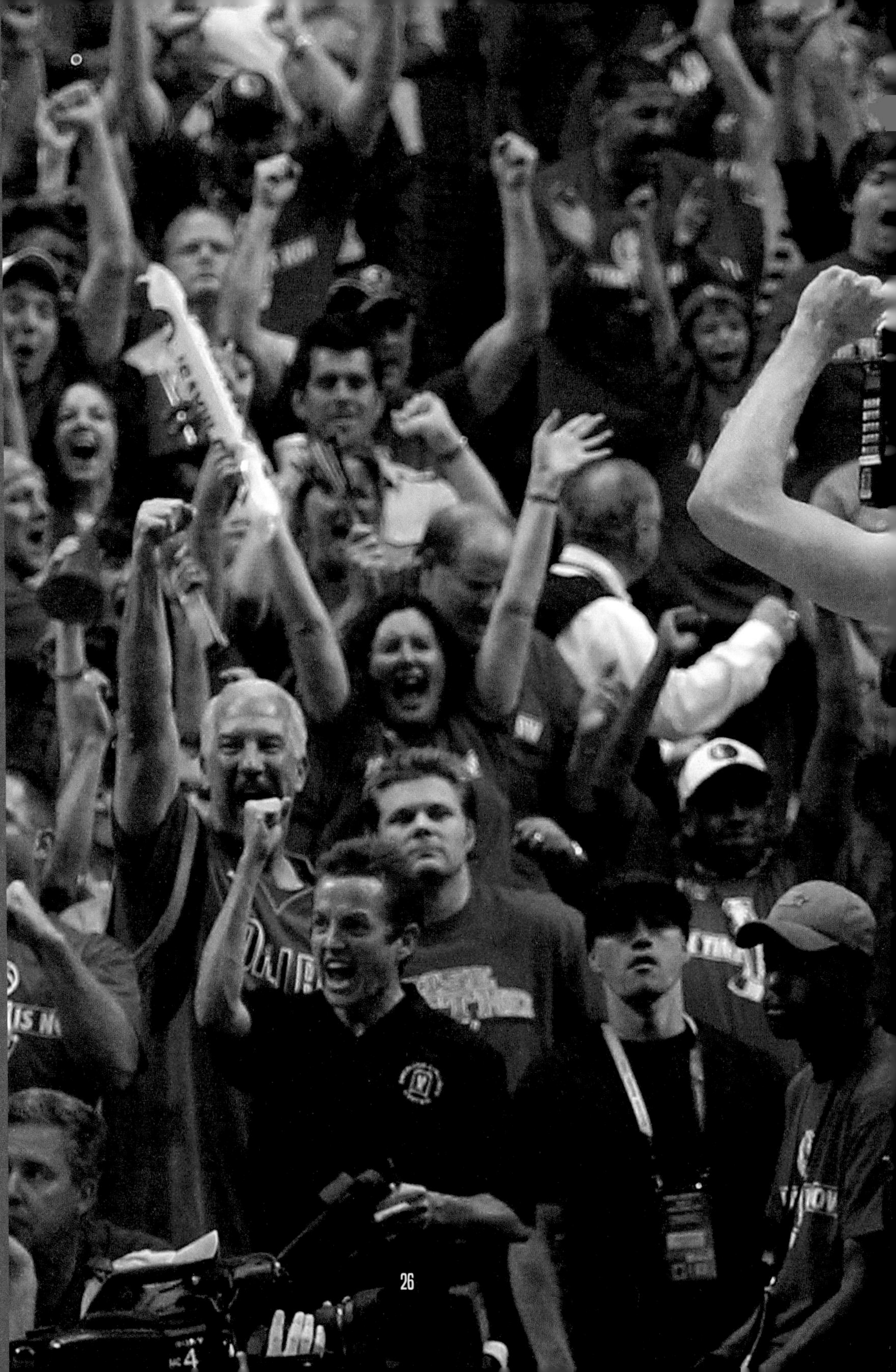

helped the Cavs to the championship in 2016.

The NBA continued to add talent. This included many players from around the world, where the league had become a global phenomenon. In 2020, the three All-NBA teams included players from Cameroon, France, Greece, Serbia, and Slovenia. That diversity set the stage for the NBA to become a truly global league as it entered its eighth decade.

TEAM HISTORY

The Hawks' history dates back to the Buffalo Bisons, which joined the NBL in 1946. Just 13 games into its first season, the team moved to Moline, Illinois. The team's name was changed to the Tri-City Blackhawks. Three years later, Tri-City was one of 17 teams to play

Trae Young (11) heads for the basket during Game 6 of the NBA Eastern Conference finals in 2021.

in the NBA's first season. In 1951, the team moved to Milwaukee. Its nickname was shortened to Hawks. Their stay in Milwaukee was brief. It was just four years before the Hawks were on the move again, this time to St. Louis, Missouri. In St. Louis, the Hawks became one of the NBA's top teams. They made the playoffs 12 times in 13 seasons and won the NBA title in 1958. But not many fans were showing up to games. In 1968, the owners decided to sell the Hawks to a group from Georgia. That group moved the team to Atlanta, where the Hawks have played ever since.

GREATEST PLAYERS

- **Zelmo Beaty**, C (1962–69)
- **Mookie Blaylock**, G (1992–99)
- **John Drew**, G-F (1974–82)
- **Cliff Hagan**, G-F (1956–66)
- **Al Horford**, C (2007–16)
- **Lou Hudson**, F-G (1966–77)
- **Joe Johnson**, G-F (2005–12)
- **Dikembe Mutombo**, C (1996–2001)
- **Bob Pettit**, F (1954–65)
- **Doc Rivers**, G (1983–91)
- **Tree Rollins**, C (1977–88)
- **Lenny Wilkens**, G (1960–68)
- **Dominique Wilkins**, F (1982–94)
- **Kevin Willis**, F-C (1984–94, 2004–05)
- **Trae Young**, G (2018–)

SLAM DUNKS

As much as anything in the 1980s, the Hawks were known for dunking. Dominique Wilkins won the NBA's second-ever Slam Dunk Contest in 1985. He also won it in 1990. In 1986, Wilkins finished second, but another Atlanta player took first place. That player was 5-foot-6 guard Anthony "Spud" Webb. He played in the NBA from 1985 to 1998. Seven of those seasons were in Atlanta.

TEAM STATS AND RECORDS*

ALL-TIME RECORD

- **Regular season:** 2,807–2,884
- **Postseason:** 165–214; one NBA title

TOP COACHES

- **Richie Guerin** (1964–72); 327–291 (regular season); 26–34 (postseason)
- **Mike Fratello** (1981, 1983–90); 324–253 (regular season); 18–22 (postseason)

CAREER LEADERS

- **Games:** Dominique Wilkins, 882
- **Points:** Dominique Wilkins, 23,292
- **Rebounds:** Bob Pettit, 12,849
- **Assists:** Doc Rivers, 3,866
- **Steals:** Mookie Blaylock, 1,321
- **Blocked shots:** Tree Rollins, 2,283

* All statistics and records in this book are through the 2020–21 season.

Dominique Wilkins (21) starred for the Hawks for 12 seasons but was never able to carry the team past the second round of the playoffs.

St. Louis Hawks forward Bob Pettit (9) leaps to shoot against the Cincinnati Royals in a 1957 game.

GREATEST SEASONS

The St. Louis Hawks reached the NBA Finals four times in five seasons, starting in 1956–57. Each time they faced the Boston Celtics, but they won the NBA title just once. That was in 1957–58, when St. Louis beat Boston in six games. The Hawks' average margin of victory in the series was just two points. Hall of Famer Bob Pettit averaged 29.3 points and 17 rebounds to lead St. Louis. In Game 6, Pettit poured in 50 points, including a tip-in with 15 seconds to play. That gave the Hawks a 110–109 victory and their only NBA title.

BOSTON CELTICS

TEAM HISTORY

The Celtics were one of 11 founding members of the BAA in 1946. They weren't very good, but they survived long enough to take part in the merger that created the NBA. Soon they began building a dynasty. The Celtics won NBA titles every decade from the 1950s to the 1980s. Through 2021, they'd won just one title in the previous 35 years. But they're still known for their green uniforms, parquet floor, and passionate fans.

Bill Russell led the NBA in rebounding four times.

GREATEST PLAYERS

- **Larry Bird**, F (1979–92)
- **Bob Cousy**, G (1950–63)
- **Dave Cowens**, C-F (1970–80)
- **Kevin Garnett**, F (2007–13)
- **John Havlicek**, F-G (1962–78)
- **Tom Heinsohn**, F-C (1956–65)
- **Dennis Johnson**, G (1983–90)
- **Sam Jones**, G-F (1957–69)
- **Kevin McHale**, F-C (1980–93)
- **Robert Parish**, C (1980–94)
- **Paul Pierce**, F (1999–2013)
- **Bill Russell**, C (1956–69)
- **Bill Sharman**, G (1951–61)
- **Jayson Tatum**, F (2017–)
- **Jo Jo White**, G (1969–79)

PRINCES OF THE PARQUET

While many NBA teams were moving into new arenas in the 1970s and later, the Celtics had tradition on their side. They stayed in a home that was built in 1928.

The Boston Garden housed both the Celtics and the Boston Bruins of the National Hockey League. It was famous not only for the legendary sporting events played there, but also for its unique court. The Celtics played on a parquet floor. It looked like puzzle pieces cut into equal-size squares. The Garden floor was unlike any other in the NBA.

The Celtics moved into a new arena, now known as TD Garden, in 1995. To maintain tradition, that arena also features a multisquared parquet floor. The Boston Garden was demolished in the late 1990s.

TEAM STATS AND RECORDS

ALL-TIME RECORD
- **Regular season:** 3,462–2,406
- **Postseason:** 382–293; 17 NBA titles

TOP COACHES
- **Red Auerbach** (1950–66); 795–397 (regular season); 90–58, nine NBA titles (postseason)
- **Tom Heinsohn** (1969–78); 427–263 (regular season); 47–33, two NBA titles (postseason)

CAREER LEADERS
- **Games:** John Havlicek, 1,270
- **Points:** John Havlicek, 26,395
- **Rebounds:** Bill Russell, 21,620
- **Assists:** Bob Cousy, 6,945
- **Steals:** Paul Pierce, 1,583
- **Blocked shots:** Robert Parish, 1,703

Paul Pierce helped return the Celtics to their winning ways during the early 2000s.

GREATEST SEASONS

The powerhouse Celtics teams that won 11 titles between 1957 and 1969 get a lot of attention, and rightfully so. But the 1980s Celtics teams that won three NBA championships thrived while facing some of the toughest competition in any era. The Hall of Fame trio of center Robert Parish and forwards Larry Bird and Kevin McHale led the way. The Celtics had excellent role players during that era as well. Forward Cedric Maxwell and guard Gerald Henderson played key roles on the 1981 and 1984 title teams. Guard Dennis Johnson and center Bill Walton helped the Celtics roll to the 1986 title. Most of the Celtics' 1980s playoff appearances were against Julius Erving and the Philadelphia 76ers or Magic Johnson's Los Angeles Lakers.

Larry Bird, *left*, and Kevin McHale, *right*, celebrate a 1986 playoff victory.

TEAM HISTORY

The Nets began play as the New Jersey Americans of the ABA in 1967. In their second season, they moved to Long Island and changed their name to the New York Nets. After struggling for a few years, the Nets added electric young forward Julius Erving to their team. He led the team to two ABA titles. In 1976, the ABA folded, but the Nets were one of four teams invited to join the NBA. They moved back to New Jersey a year later and played there until 2012. Then they moved to an arena in Brooklyn, New York.

GREATEST PLAYERS

- **Kenny Anderson**, G (1991–96)
- **Vince Carter**, G-F (2004–09)
- **Derrick Coleman**, F (1990–95)
- **Kevin Durant**, F (2020–)
- **Julius Erving**, F-G (1973–76)
- **James Harden**, G (2021–)
- **Kyrie Irving**, G (2019–)
- **Richard Jefferson**, F (2001–08)
- **Jason Kidd**, G (2001–08)
- **Brook Lopez**, C (2008–17)
- **Bill Melchionni**, G (1969–76)
- **Billy Paultz**, C-F (1970–75)
- **Drazen Petrovic**, G (1991–93)
- **Buck Williams**, F-C (1981–89)
- **Deron Williams**, G (2011–15)

Kevin Durant takes a shot during a 2021 playoff game against the Milwaukee Bucks.

TEAM STATS AND RECORDS

ALL-TIME RECORD

- **Regular season**: 1,907–2,459
- **Postseason**: 70–93; two ABA titles

TOP COACHES

- **Kevin Loughery** (1973–80); 297–318 (regular season); 21–13, two ABA titles (postseason)
- **Lawrence Frank** (2004–10); 225–241 (regular season); 18–20 (postseason)

CAREER LEADERS

- **Games**: Buck Williams, 635
- **Points**: Brook Lopez, 10,444
- **Rebounds**: Buck Williams, 7,576
- **Assists**: Jason Kidd, 4,620
- **Steals**: Jason Kidd, 950
- **Blocked shots**: Brook Lopez, 972

Julius Erving rises for one of his trademark dunks. The Nets won the ABA title in 1974 in Erving's first season with the team.

GREATEST SEASONS

The Nets won the ABA title in 1974 and did it again in 1976. Erving was their star. He led the league in scoring in both his team's championship seasons. But he got help from plenty of teammates. The 1974 team featured rugged center Billy Paultz and power forward Larry Kenon. The Nets coasted through the playoffs, losing just two games in three series. Two years later, guards Brian Taylor and John Williamson each averaged more than 16 points per game. The Nets edged the San Antonio Spurs in seven games and the Denver Nuggets in six to earn their second title.

The Nets' Brian Taylor, *left*, defends the Spurs' George Gervin during Game 7 of the 1976 ABA semifinals. New York prevailed 121–114.

JULIUS ERVING

Julius Erving grew up in Roosevelt, New York, not far from where the Nets played in Uniondale. Joining the Nets in 1973 was like a homecoming for him. Erving played five seasons in the ABA. The former University of Massachusetts standout spent his first two professional seasons with the ABA's Virginia Squires before he joined the Nets. Erving won three scoring titles and three MVP Awards in the ABA. After the ABA and the NBA merged, he played 11 seasons in the NBA with the Philadelphia 76ers.

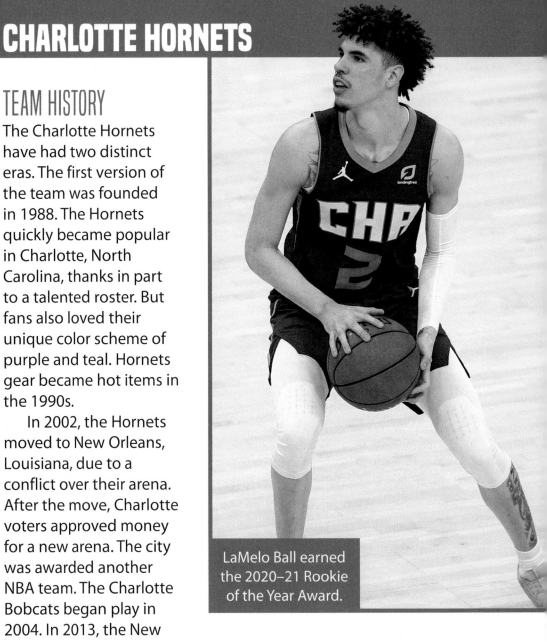

LaMelo Ball earned the 2020–21 Rookie of the Year Award.

TEAM HISTORY

The Charlotte Hornets have had two distinct eras. The first version of the team was founded in 1988. The Hornets quickly became popular in Charlotte, North Carolina, thanks in part to a talented roster. But fans also loved their unique color scheme of purple and teal. Hornets gear became hot items in the 1990s.

In 2002, the Hornets moved to New Orleans, Louisiana, due to a conflict over their arena. After the move, Charlotte voters approved money for a new arena. The city was awarded another NBA team. The Charlotte Bobcats began play in 2004. In 2013, the New Orleans Hornets decided to change their name to the Pelicans. The next year, the Bobcats returned to their roots. They reclaimed the Hornets nickname for Charlotte. However, the team hasn't found much success. It made the playoffs just three times in its first 16 seasons. It lost in the first round each time.

GREATEST PLAYERS

- **Tyrone Bogues**, G (1988–97)
- **Rex Chapman**, G (1988–92)
- **Dell Curry**, G-F (1988–98)
- **Al Jefferson**, C (2013–16)
- **Larry Johnson**, F (1991–96)
- **Anthony Mason**, F (1996–98, 1999–2000)
- **Alonzo Mourning**, C (1992–95)

- **Emeka Okafor**, F-C (2004–09)
- **J. R. Reid**, F-C (1989–92, 1997–99)
- **Glen Rice**, F (1995–98)
- **Kelly Tripucka**, F (1988–91)
- **Kemba Walker**, G (2011–19)
- **Gerald Wallace**, F (2004–11)
- **Marvin Williams**, F (2014–20)
- **Cody Zeller**, C (2013–21)

PRESIDENT MICHAEL JORDAN

Michael Jordan served as the Bobcats' president from 2006 to 2010. He became the team's primary owner in 2010. The Hall of Fame guard grew up in Wilmington, North Carolina. He played in college at the University of North Carolina. While playing for the Chicago Bulls, Jordan led the team to six NBA titles in the 1990s. He won six NBA Finals MVP Awards, while leading the NBA in scoring ten times. Jordan was also president of the Washington Wizards from 2000 to 2002.

Emeka Okafor (50) grabs a rebound in 2004.

41

TEAM STATS AND RECORDS

ALL-TIME RECORD

- **Regular season:** 1,083–1,384
- **Postseason:** 23–40

TOP COACHES

- **Allan Bristow** (1991–96); 207–203 (regular season); 5–8 (postseason)
- **Steve Clifford** (2013–18); 196–214 (regular season); 3–8 (postseason)

CAREER LEADERS

- **Games:** Dell Curry, 701
- **Points:** Kemba Walker, 12,009
- **Rebounds:** Emeka Okafor, 3,516
- **Assists:** Muggsy Bogues, 5,557
- **Steals:** Muggsy Bogues, 1,067
- **Blocked shots:** Alonzo Mourning, 684

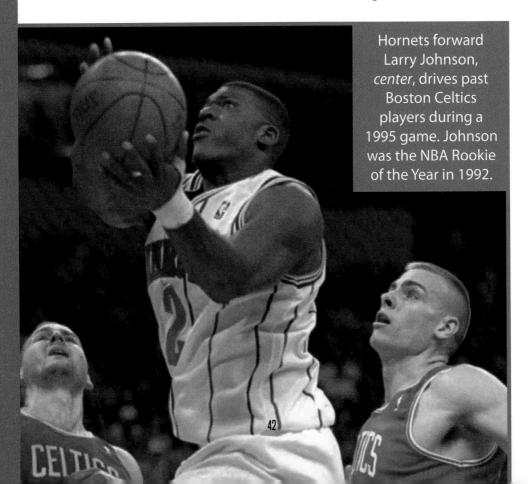

Hornets forward Larry Johnson, *center*, drives past Boston Celtics players during a 1995 game. Johnson was the NBA Rookie of the Year in 1992.

GREATEST SEASONS

The Hornets of the early 1990s had some of the game's most exciting young players. Center Alonzo Mourning and forward Larry Johnson led the way. Guard Dell Curry was a mainstay off the bench. And 5-foot-3 point guard Muggsy Bogues was a fan favorite throughout the league. The Hornets reached the playoffs four times from 1993 to 1998. They got to the Eastern Conference semifinals twice.

Charlotte center Alonzo Mourning, *back left*, holds the ball over two Knicks players in a 1993 playoff game.

TEAM HISTORY

The Bulls debuted in the 1966–67 season. They had some early success, making the playoffs eight times in their first nine seasons. However, they didn't win a playoff series until 1974. The next year they came up one game shy of reaching the NBA Finals. That was their high-water mark until Michael Jordan came along a decade later. He turned the Bulls into a machine, winning six NBA titles in eight years. Through 2021, the team had reached the conference finals only once since Jordan left.

Zach LaVine drives to the basket during a 2021 game.

GREATEST PLAYERS

- **Jimmy Butler**, G-F (2011–17)
- **Luol Deng**, F (2004–14)
- **Artis Gilmore**, C (1976–82, 1987)
- **Horace Grant**, F-C (1987–94)
- **Kirk Hinrich**, G (2003–10, 2012–16)
- **Michael Jordan**, G-F (1984–93, 1995–98)
- **Zach LaVine**, G (2017–)
- **Bob Love**, F (1968–76)
- **Joakim Noah**, C (2007–16)
- **John Paxson**, G (1985–94)
- **Scottie Pippen**, F-G (1987–98, 2003–04)
- **Dennis Rodman**, F (1995–98)
- **Derrick Rose**, G (2008–12, 2013–16)
- **Jerry Sloan**, G (1966–76)
- **Chet Walker**, F (1969–75)

Chicago native Derrick Rose helped make the Bulls competitive again after they picked him first overall in the 2008 draft.

TEAM STATS AND RECORDS

ALL-TIME RECORD

- **Regular season:** 2,258–2,176
- **Postseason:** 186–158; six NBA titles

TOP COACHES

- **Dick Motta** (1968–76); 356–300 (regular season); 18–29 (postseason)
- **Phil Jackson** (1989–98); 545–193 (regular season); 111–41, six NBA titles (postseason)

CAREER LEADERS

- **Games:** Michael Jordan, 930
- **Points:** Michael Jordan, 29,277
- **Rebounds:** Michael Jordan, 5,836
- **Assists:** Michael Jordan, 5,012
- **Steals:** Michael Jordan, 2,306
- **Blocked shots:** Artis Gilmore, 1,029

JACKSON'S IMPACT

Phil Jackson enjoyed a solid 12-year playing career with the New York Knicks and New Jersey Nets. That included winning an NBA title in 1973. However, Jackson really found his calling as a coach. Before the 1989–90 season, Jackson was named the Bulls' head coach. In nine seasons with the Bulls, he led them to six championships. Chicago won at least 47 games in each of his seasons there.

Jackson then went on to coach the Los Angeles Lakers. In the 2009–10 season, the Lakers won their fifth title in 11 years with Jackson. By the time Jackson retired after the 2010–11 season, he had more championship rings than he had fingers to wear them. His 11 NBA titles as head coach were unmatched. Jackson entered the Basketball Hall of Fame in 2007.

GREATEST SEASONS

The Bulls beat the Los Angeles Lakers in the 1991 NBA Finals, starting a string of three straight championships. Jordan then retired to pursue a professional baseball career. He missed almost two full seasons. The Bulls fell short of the conference finals both years. After Jordan's return, they again won three consecutive titles, starting with the 1995–96 team that set an NBA record at the time with 72 regular-season victories.

In addition to leading the Bulls to six NBA titles, Michael Jordan drew attention for his massive dunks during the league's Slam Dunk Contests.

CLEVELAND CAVALIERS

TEAM HISTORY

The Cavaliers joined the NBA in 1970. Aside from a run to the Eastern Conference finals in 1976, the Cavs were one of the worst teams in the league for their first two decades. They became a frequent playoff participant in the 1990s, but it took the arrival of LeBron James in 2003 for them really compete for the NBA title. With James on board, Cleveland reached the playoffs for five straight seasons. The Cavs won at least one series each year and reached the NBA Finals in 2007. After James left in 2010, Cleveland averaged fewer than 25 wins the next four years. Then James returned and led them to four straight Eastern Conference titles and their only NBA title.

GREATEST PLAYERS

- **Terrell Brandon**, G (1991–97)
- **Austin Carr**, G (1971–80)
- **Brad Daugherty**, C (1986–94)
- **World B. Free**, G (1982–86)
- **Zydrunas Ilgauskas**, C (1997–2010)
- **Kyrie Irving**, G (2011–17)
- **LeBron James**, G-F (2003–10, 2014–18)
- **Kevin Love**, F (2014–)
- **Mike Mitchell**, F (1978–81)
- **Larry Nance**, F (1988–94)
- **Mark Price**, G (1986–95)
- **Robert "Bingo" Smith**, F (1970–79)
- **Tristan Thompson**, F-C (2011–20)
- **Anderson Varejão**, C (2004–16, 2021)
- **John Williams**, F (1986–95)

Collin Sexton (2) dribbles past a Washington forward.

THE BEST BEFORE JAMES?

Who is the best player in Cavaliers history aside from LeBron James? Many people have debated that question. A frequent choice is Mark Price. Price averaged between 15 and 20 points a game every season from 1987–88 to 1994–95. He was also one of the finest foul shooters in NBA history and a great passer. Until James arrived in 2003, Price was the only player in Cavaliers history to be named to the All-NBA first team. He earned that honor in 1993 after averaging 18.2 points and eight assists per game. He also led the league by hitting nearly 95 percent of his foul shots.

TEAM STATS AND RECORDS

ALL-TIME RECORD

- **Regular season:** 1,889–2,218
- **Postseason:** 125–104; one NBA title

TOP COACHES

- **Lenny Wilkens** (1986–93); 316–258 (regular season); 18–23 (postseason)
- **Mike Brown** (2005–10, 2013–14); 305–187 (regular season); 42–29 (postseason)
- **Tyronn Lue** (2016–18); 128–83 (regular season); 41–20, one NBA title (postseason)

CAREER LEADERS

- **Games:** LeBron James, 849
- **Points:** LeBron James, 23,119
- **Rebounds:** LeBron James, 6,190
- **Assists:** LeBron James, 6,228
- **Steals:** LeBron James, 1,376
- **Blocked shots:** Zydrunas Ilgauskas, 1,269

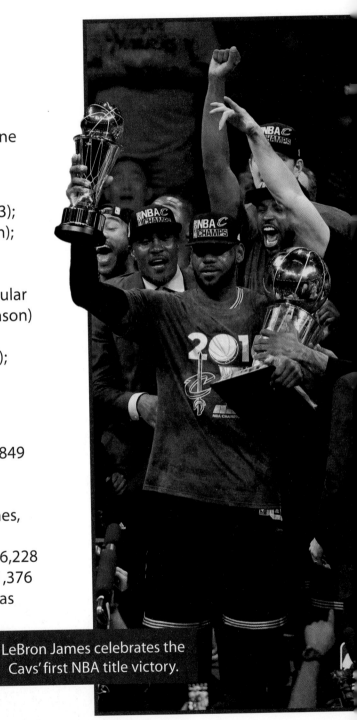

LeBron James celebrates the Cavs' first NBA title victory.

GREATEST SEASONS

In 2014, James returned to the Cavs from his four-year stay with the Miami Heat. He immediately went to work trying to bring a championship to his hometown team. The Cavs reached the NBA Finals in each of the next four seasons. They faced the Golden State Warriors for the title each year, and they lost three times. But in the 2016 NBA Finals, they made history. After losing three of the first four games, the Cavs rallied to win three straight to take the title. No NBA team had ever come back from a 3–1 deficit in the Finals. The team clinched the title with a thrilling Game 7 victory on the road, as guard Kyrie Irving hit a late three-pointer to break an 89–89 tie.

Anderson Varejão snags the ball during a 2010 game against the Philadelphia 76ers.

TEAM HISTORY

The Mavericks joined the NBA in 1980. They were one of the worst teams in league history their first year, winning just 15 games. But by their fourth season they were a playoff team, reaching the postseason six times in seven years. The 1990s were pretty lean, but the addition of forward Dirk Nowitzki in 1998 made them an instant threat. They reached the NBA Finals in 2006 but lost to the Miami Heat. The teams met in a rematch five years later. That time the Mavs prevailed to win their first NBA title.

Guard Luka Dončić emerged as one of the NBA's brightest stars upon his debut with the Mavs in 2018.

52

GREATEST PLAYERS

- **Mark Aguirre**, F (1981–89)
- **Rolando Blackman**, G (1981–92)
- **Brad Davis**, G (1980–92)
- **James Donaldson**, C (1985–92)
- **Luka Dončić**, G (2018–)
- **Michael Finley**, G-F (1996–2005)
- **Derek Harper**, G (1983–94, 1996–97)
- **Jim Jackson**, G (1992–97)
- **Jason Kidd**, G (1994–96, 2008–12)
- **Jamal Mashburn**, F (1993–97)
- **Steve Nash**, G (1999–2004)
- **Dirk Nowitzki**, F (1998–2019)
- **Sam Perkins**, F-C (1984–90)
- **Roy Tarpley**, F-C (1986–90, 1994–95)
- **Jay Vincent**, F (1981–86)

SLOVENIAN SUPERSTAR

European players have made significant contributions to the NBA. Luka Dončić, who was born in Slovenia, is one of them. At age 13, he signed a contract to play for the Spanish basketball club Real Madrid. He was just 16 when he became the youngest player ever to crack the lineup of the club's senior team. Three years later, he led Real Madrid to the EuroLeague title. He earned MVP honors for both the regular season and the Final Four. But Dončić was just getting started. Shortly after winning the EuroLeague championship, he was the third pick in the 2018 NBA Draft. It didn't take him long to make a huge impact with the Mavericks. The 6-foot-7 guard found that his size and skills were a perfect fit with the American version of the game. He averaged 21.2 points, 7.8 rebounds, and six assists per game. He also received the NBA Rookie of the Year Award.

TEAM STATS AND RECORDS

ALL-TIME RECORD

- **Regular season:** 1,657–1,640
- **Postseason:** 96–113; one NBA title

TOP COACHES

- **Don Nelson** (1997–2005); 339–251 (regular season); 19–24 (postseason)
- **Rick Carlisle** (2008–21); 555–478 (regular season); 33–38, one NBA title (postseason)

CAREER LEADERS

- **Games:** Dirk Nowitzki, 1,522
- **Points:** Dirk Nowitzki, 31,560
- **Rebounds:** Dirk Nowitzki, 11,489
- **Assists:** Derek Harper, 5,111
- **Steals:** Derek Harper, 1,551
- **Blocked shots:** Dirk Nowitzki, 1,281

Mavs forward Dirk Nowitzki, *left*, keeps the ball from Spurs player Bruce Bowen during a playoff game in 2006.

The Mavs and head coach Rick Carlisle celebrate their first NBA title after defeating the Miami Heat in 2011.

GREATEST SEASONS

At age 32, Nowitzki's prime years were behind him. But he still had enough in the tank to lead the 2010–11 Mavericks to the NBA Finals for the second time. He wasn't the only veteran to play a big role for Dallas that season. Point guard Jason Kidd was 38 years old. He led the team in assists. Guard Jason Terry, 33, and forwards Shawn Marion, 33, and Caron Butler, 31, were the team's top three scorers after Nowitzki. In the NBA Finals, they faced the Miami Heat in Miami's first year with LeBron James, Dwyane Wade, and Chris Bosh in the lineup. Miami took two of the first three games. But the veteran Mavericks won the next three to bring an NBA title to Dallas.

TEAM HISTORY

The Denver Rockets were founding members of the ABA in 1967. Denver had one of the league's most consistent teams, reaching the ABA playoffs in each of the league's nine seasons. In 1974, they changed their name to the Nuggets to avoid being confused with the NBA's Houston Rockets. The Nuggets reached the ABA Finals in the league's final season, losing to Julius Erving's New York Nets. Then they became one of four ABA teams that joined the NBA in 1976. They remained a regular playoff participant after that, especially once center Nikola Jokić arrived in 2015. However, through 2021 they had not made it back to the league finals.

GREATEST PLAYERS

- **Carmelo Anthony**, F (2003–11)
- **Byron Beck**, C-F (1967–77)
- **Chauncey Billups**, G (1999–2000, 2008–11)
- **T. R. Dunn**, G-F (1980–88, 1989–90)
- **Alex English**, F (1979–90)
- **Bill Hanzlik**, G-F (1982–90)
- **Dan Issel**, C-F (1975–85)
- **Nikola Jokić**, C (2015–)
- **Bobby Jones**, F (1974–78)
- **Fat Lever**, G (1984–90)
- **Jamal Murray**, G (2016–)
- **Dikembe Mutombo**, C (1991–96)
- **Nenê**, C-F (2002–12)
- **David Thompson**, G-F (1975–82)
- **Kiki Vandeweghe**, F (1980–84)

Nikola Jokić earned the
2020–21 MVP Award.

TEAM STATS AND RECORDS

ALL-TIME RECORD

- **Regular season:** 2,209–2,158
- **Postseason:** 81–124

TOP COACHES

- **Doug Moe** (1980–90); 432–357 (regular season); 24–37 (postseason)
- **George Karl** (2005–13); 423–257 (regular season); 21–38 (postseason)

CAREER LEADERS

- **Games:** Alex English, 837
- **Points:** Alex English, 21,645
- **Rebounds:** Dan Issel, 6,630
- **Assists:** Alex English, 3,679
- **Steals:** Fat Lever, 1,167
- **Blocked shots:** Dikembe Mutombo, 1,486

The Nuggets' Dikembe Mutombo (55) spins around Seattle's Michael Cage during the 1994 Western Conference playoffs.

GREATEST SEASONS

The 1975–76 Nuggets had a tough act to follow. The previous season they'd won 65 games—a mark that remains a team record—and reached the conference finals. They lost a seven-game series to the Indiana Pacers. But they added a dynamic young guard from North Carolina State University named David Thompson. The high-flying Thompson finished third in the league in scoring as a rookie.

David Thompson, *left*, averaged more than 24 points per game in seven seasons with the Nuggets.

The Nuggets had the league's best record at the All-Star break, so they faced a team composed of the best players from the rest of the league at that year's All-Star Game. At halftime, Thompson took part in the first Slam Dunk Contest, which would become a fan favorite in the NBA. And he led a fourth-quarter comeback to win the game's MVP Award as the Nuggets beat the All-Stars 144–138.

A QUIET STAR

No conversation about the greatest players in Nuggets history could be complete without Alex English. English was a standout at the University of South Carolina before the Milwaukee Bucks drafted him in 1976. The lanky 6-foot-7 forward played two unremarkable seasons in Milwaukee before he signed with the Indiana Pacers. English began to score more points, but it was not until he was traded to Denver during the 1979–80 season that he developed into a star.

While with the Nuggets, English became known for his elegant style of play, his midrange shooting ability, and his unassuming way of doing his job. He led the NBA in scoring during the 1982–83 season at 28.4 points per game. English averaged at least 25 points in eight straight seasons beginning in 1981–82. Through 2021, his 21,645 points ranked first in club history.

TEAM HISTORY

The Pistons were founded in Fort Wayne, Indiana, in 1941. They reached the NBL Finals for two straight years in the mid-1940s before joining the NBA in 1949. In 1957, they moved to Detroit, Michigan. The team's owner realized he needed to go to a larger city to increase game attendance. That way, the Pistons could keep up with the other teams in the NBA. The Pistons won back-to-back NBA titles in 1989 and 1990. They added a third trophy in 2004. But then the team fell on hard times. Through 2021, they had made the playoffs just twice in the previous 12 seasons.

Cade Cunningham takes a shot over a Houston Rockets player during a 2021 game.

GREATEST PLAYERS

- **Chauncey Billups**, G (2002–08)
- **Dave Bing**, G (1966–75)
- **Dave DeBusschere**, F-G (1962–68)
- **Andre Drummond**, C (2012–20)
- **Joe Dumars**, G (1985–99)
- **Blake Griffin**, F (2018–21)
- **Richard Hamilton**, G (2002–11)
- **Grant Hill**, G-F (1994–2000)
- **Bill Laimbeer**, C (1982–93)
- **Bob Lanier**, C (1970–80)
- **Tayshaun Prince**, F (2002–13, 2015)
- **Dennis Rodman**, F (1986–93)
- **Isiah Thomas**, G (1981–94)
- **Ben Wallace**, C (2001–06, 2009–12)
- **George Yardley**, F (1953–59)

Pistons forward Dennis Rodman pulls down a rebound during a 1993 game. Rodman led the NBA with 18.3 rebounds per game that season.

TEAM STATS AND RECORDS

ALL-TIME RECORD
- **Regular season:** 2,773–2,979
- **Postseason:** 188–182; three NBA titles

TOP COACHES
- **Chuck Daly** (1983–92); 467–271 (regular season); 71–42, two NBA titles (postseason)
- **Flip Saunders** (2005–08); 176–70 (regular season); 30–21 (postseason)

CAREER LEADERS
- **Games**: Joe Dumars, 1,018
- **Points**: Isiah Thomas, 18,822
- **Rebounds**: Bill Laimbeer, 9,430
- **Assists**: Isiah Thomas, 9,061
- **Steals**: Isiah Thomas, 1,861
- **Blocked shots**: Ben Wallace, 1,486

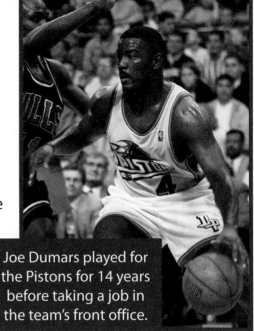

Joe Dumars played for the Pistons for 14 years before taking a job in the team's front office.

A MULTITALENTED ATHLETE

Dave DeBusschere grew up on Detroit's East Side. He was a star football, baseball, and basketball player. In college, he played for the University of Detroit's baseball and basketball teams. In 1962, the Pistons selected him in the NBA Draft. The Chicago White Sox also signed him to play baseball. DeBusschere decided to pursue both sports. He played for the Pistons and also for the White Sox and their minor league clubs. In 1966, he turned his focus to basketball. DeBusschere was voted into the Basketball Hall of Fame in 1983.

GREATEST SEASONS

The Pistons teams of the late 1980s were called the Bad Boys because they played a tough—some might even say dirty—style of basketball. Center Bill Laimbeer and forwards Rick Mahorn and Dennis Rodman provided most of the muscle. Detroit's talented backcourt featured point guard Isiah Thomas and shooting guard Joe Dumars, both future Hall of Famers. Their toughest challenges in the playoffs came from Michael Jordan's Chicago Bulls. The Pistons edged the Bulls in the conference finals in six games in 1989 and in seven games the next year. After passing those tests, they swept the Los Angeles Lakers in 1989 to win one title. In 1990, they beat the Portland Trail Blazers in five games to win it again.

Forward Dennis Rodman lifts Isiah Thomas into the air after the Pistons won Game 1 of the 1990 NBA Finals.

GOLDEN STATE WARRIORS

TEAM HISTORY

The Philadelphia Warriors were founding members of the BAA in 1946. They also won the first BAA title. They joined the NBA in 1949 when the BAA folded. They won another league title while playing in Philadelphia, Pennsylvania. In 1962, the team was sold. The new owners moved the Warriors to San Francisco, California. In the 1967–68 season, the Warriors began playing some games in a new arena across the bay in Oakland, California. Four years later, they moved to Oakland full-time. They changed their name to the Golden State Warriors. Golden State won an NBA championship in 1975, with Hall of Famer Rick Barry leading a sweep of the Washington Bullets in the Finals. Forty years later, the Warriors put together a string of great teams that brought home even more trophies.

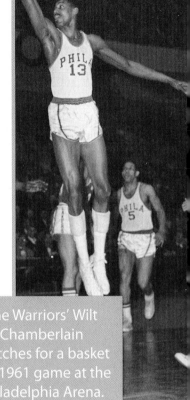

The Warriors' Wilt Chamberlain stretches for a basket in a 1961 game at the Philadelphia Arena.

WILT'S CENTURY CLUB

On March 2, 1962, Wilt Chamberlain wrote his name in the NBA record books by scoring 100 points in the Warriors' 169–147 victory over the New York Knicks. The young center regularly dominated play under the basket. But that night, he was nearly unstoppable. He made 36 of his 63 shots from the field. He also sank 28 of 32 free throws, even though on average he only made about half of his free throws during his entire career. Chamberlain's night broke his own record of 78 points in a game. Sixty years after his feat, no NBA player had come close to matching it.

GREATEST PLAYERS

- **Paul Arizin**, G-F (1950–52, 1954–62)
- **Rick Barry**, F (1965–67, 1972–78)
- **Wilt Chamberlain**, C (1959–65)
- **Stephen Curry**, G (2009–)
- **Kevin Durant**, F (2016–19)
- **Monta Ellis**, G (2005–12)
- **Joe Fulks**, F-C (1946–54)

- **Draymond Green**, F (2012–)
- **Tim Hardaway**, G (1989–96)
- **Neil Johnston**, C (1951–59)
- **Chris Mullin**, G-F (1985–97, 2000–01)
- **Robert Parish**, C (1976–80)
- **Purvis Short**, G-F (1978–87)
- **Klay Thompson**, G (2011–)
- **Nate Thurmond**, F-C (1963–74)

The Warriors' Chris Mullin goes up for a shot in 1997. Mullin was named to the Basketball Hall of Fame in 2011.

TEAM STATS AND RECORDS

ALL-TIME RECORD

- **Regular season**: 2,826–3,031
- **Postseason**: 190–159; six NBA titles

TOP COACHES

- **Al Attles** (1970–83); 557–518 (regular season); 31–30, one NBA title (postseason)
- **Don Nelson** (1988–95, 2006–10); 422–443 (regular season); 14–21 (postseason)
- **Steve Kerr** (2014–); 376–171 (regular season); 77–28, three NBA titles (postseason)

CAREER LEADERS

- **Games**: Chris Mullin, 807
- **Points**: Stephen Curry, 18,434
- **Rebounds**: Nate Thurmond, 12,771
- **Assists**: Stephen Curry, 4,984
- **Steals**: Chris Mullin, 1,360
- **Blocked shots**: Adonal Foyle, 1,140

GREATEST SEASONS

The Warriors won five straight Western Conference titles beginning in 2014–15. They won the NBA Finals after three of those seasons, beating the Cleveland Cavaliers each time. Guards Stephen Curry and Klay Thompson were the leaders of those dynamic, high-scoring squads. In 2015–16, they set the NBA record for regular-season wins with 73. But they lost a dramatic seven-game Finals series to the Cavs that year.

Klay Thompson, Stephen Curry, and Andre Iguodala, *from left to right*, celebrate during a 2019 playoff game.

TEAM HISTORY

The San Diego Rockets began play in 1967. They spent four years in Southern California and made the playoffs once. In 1971, the team moved to Houston, Texas. The Rockets had some success in the 1980s. They made the NBA Finals twice, losing to the Boston Celtics both times. They won back-to-back titles in the mid-1990s and have enjoyed a strong rivalry with the two other Texas teams—San Antonio and Dallas—throughout the years.

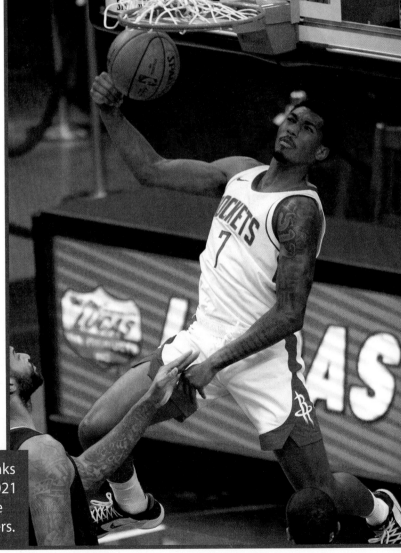

Armoni Brooks dunks the ball during a 2021 game against the Los Angeles Clippers.

Rockets center Yao Ming guards San Antonio Spurs center David Robinson during Yao's NBA debut in October 2002.

GREATEST PLAYERS

- **Clint Capela**, C (2014–20)
- **Steve Francis**, G (1999–2004, 2007)
- **James Harden**, G (2012–21)
- **Elvin Hayes**, C (1968–72, 1981–84)
- **Robert Horry**, F (1992–96)
- **Moses Malone**, C (1976–82)
- **Tracy McGrady**, G-F (2004–10)
- **Yao Ming**, C (2002–11)
- **Calvin Murphy**, G (1970–83)
- **Hakeem Olajuwon**, F-C (1984–2001)
- **Robert Reid**, F-G (1977–88)
- **Ralph Sampson**, C (1983–87)
- **Kenny Smith**, G (1990–96)
- **Otis Thorpe**, F (1988–95)
- **Rudy Tomjanovich**, F (1970–81)

TEAM STATS AND RECORDS

ALL-TIME RECORD
- **Regular season**: 2,286–2,074
- **Postseason**: 158–164; two NBA titles

TOP COACHES
- **Rudy Tomjanovich** (1992–2003); 503–397 (regular season); 51–39, two NBA titles (postseason)
- **Mike D'Antoni** (2016–20); 217–101 (regular season); 28–23 (postseason)

CAREER LEADERS
- **Games**: Hakeem Olajuwon, 1,177
- **Points**: Hakeem Olajuwon, 26,511
- **Rebounds**: Hakeem Olajuwon, 13,382
- **Assists**: James Harden, 4,796
- **Steals**: Hakeem Olajuwon, 2,088
- **Blocked shots**: Hakeem Olajuwon, 3,740

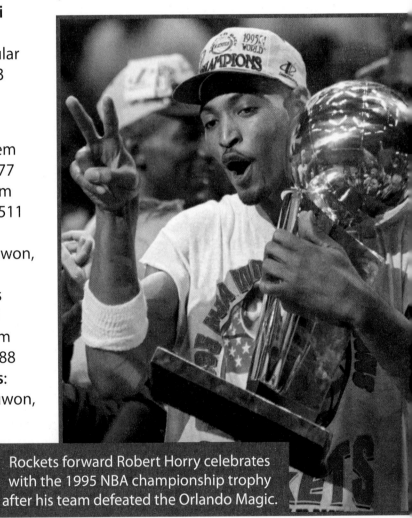

Rockets forward Robert Horry celebrates with the 1995 NBA championship trophy after his team defeated the Orlando Magic.

GREATEST SEASONS

Beginning in 1991, Michael Jordan's Bulls won the NBA title six times in eight years. The Rockets took advantage of the two years Chicago didn't win it all. Led by Hall of Fame center Hakeem Olajuwon, forward Otis Thorpe, and guard Kenny Smith, the Rockets slipped past the New York Knicks in Game 7 of the 1994 NBA Finals. The next year, Hall of Famer Clyde Drexler joined the team. The Rockets rolled to a four-game sweep of the Orlando Magic for their second straight title.

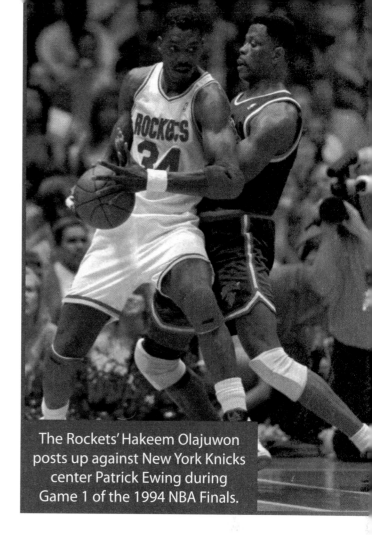

The Rockets' Hakeem Olajuwon posts up against New York Knicks center Patrick Ewing during Game 1 of the 1994 NBA Finals.

BIG-SHOT BOB

Robert Horry played the first four of his 16 NBA seasons with the Rockets. He won seven NBA titles during his career—two with Houston, three with the Los Angeles Lakers, and two with the San Antonio Spurs. A solid defender and good outside shooter, Horry earned the nickname "Big-Shot Bob" for his ability to hit the big shot when it was most needed. He helped the Rockets to the 1995 NBA Finals against the Orlando Magic. Horry was consistent throughout the Finals, averaging 17.8 points, ten rebounds, and 3.8 assists per game. In Game 2, he set an NBA Finals record with seven steals as the Rockets won 117–106.

INDIANA PACERS

TEAM HISTORY

The Pacers were founding members of the ABA in 1967. They were one of the most successful teams in the upstart league, winning titles in 1970, 1972, and 1973. They joined the NBA when the ABA folded in 1976. They came close to reaching the NBA Finals in 1994

Domantas Sabonis became a star with the Pacers after joining the team in 2017.

and 1995. However, they lost a seven-game conference finals series each year. Indiana finally got over the hump in 2000, only to lose to the Los Angeles Lakers in the NBA Finals.

GREATEST PLAYERS

- **Roger Brown**, F (1967–74, 1975)
- **Mel Daniels**, C (1968–74)
- **Antonio Davis**, F-C (1993–99)
- **Dale Davis**, F (1991–2000, 2005)
- **Vern Fleming**, G (1984–95)
- **Paul George**, G-F (2010–17)
- **Danny Granger**, F (2005–14)
- **Billy Knight**, G (1974–77, 1979–83)
- **George McGinnis**, F (1971–75, 1980–82)
- **Reggie Miller**, G (1987–2005)
- **Victor Oladipo**, G (2017–21)
- **Jermaine O'Neal**, F-C (2000–08)
- **Jalen Rose**, G (1996–2002)
- **Domantas Sabonis**, F-C (2017–)
- **Rik Smits**, C (1988–2000)

SLICK LEONARD

Bob "Slick" Leonard grew up in a working-class family in Terre Haute, Indiana. He was a star high school basketball player. He later played at Indiana University and in the NBA.

When Leonard began coaching the Pacers in 1969, he brought a tough, aggressive style. He also stressed team unity. Leonard won 529 games while coaching the Pacers for 12 years in the ABA and NBA. He later served as the team's radio and TV broadcaster. Leonard was known for saying, "Boom, baby!" each time a Pacers player hit a three-pointer.

Pacers forward George McGinnis sets the ball into the basket during a 1975 game at Market Square Arena in Indianapolis.

TEAM STATS AND RECORDS

ALL-TIME RECORD
- **Regular season:** 2,250–2,116
- **Postseason:** 115–126; three ABA titles

TOP COACHES
- **Bob "Slick" Leonard** (1968–80); 529–456 (regular season); 69–47, three ABA titles (postseason)
- **Frank Vogel** (2011–16); 250–181 (regular season); 31–30 (postseason)

CAREER LEADERS
- **Games:** Reggie Miller, 1,389
- **Points:** Reggie Miller, 25,279
- **Rebounds:** Mel Daniels, 7,643
- **Assists:** Reggie Miller, 4,141
- **Steals:** Reggie Miller, 1,505
- **Blocked shots:** Jermaine O'Neal, 1,245

GREATEST SEASONS

Future Hall of Fame forward Roger Brown helped lead the Pacers to three ABA titles in four years, starting in 1970. He had plenty of help from fellow Hall of Famer Mel Daniels, while George McGinnis led the team in scoring in the final year of their run. It could have been four straight titles, but the Pacers lost to the Utah Stars in Game 7 of the 1971 conference finals.

Reggie Miller tries to maneuver around Patrick Ewing of the New York Knicks in the 1995 Eastern Conference finals.

TEAM HISTORY

The Clippers started out in western New York in 1970 as the Buffalo Braves. The team struggled in its first few seasons. But with the emergence of star forward Bob McAdoo, the Braves made the playoffs for three straight seasons. An ownership change brought the team to San Diego, California, in 1978. The team's name changed

Kawhi Leonard dunks over a Jazz player during a 2021 playoff game.

to the San Diego Clippers. After five straight losing seasons, the Clippers moved up the coast to Los Angeles. Though they've long played in the Lakers' shadow, the Clippers ended 2021 having made the playoffs nine times in their last ten seasons.

GREATEST PLAYERS

- **Elton Brand**, F (2001–08)
- **Sam Cassell**, G (2005–08)
- **Terry Cummings**, F (1982–84)
- **Ernie DiGregorio**, G (1973–77)
- **Blake Griffin**, F (2010–18)
- **DeAndre Jordan**, C (2008–18)
- **Corey Maggette**, F (2000–08)
- **Danny Manning**, F-C (1988–94)
- **Bob McAdoo**, C-F (1972–76)
- **Swen Nater**, C (1977–83)
- **Chris Paul**, G (2011–17)
- **Charles Smith**, F-C (1988–92)
- **Randy Smith**, G (1971–79, 1982–83)
- **Loy Vaught**, F (1990–98)
- **Bill Walton**, C-F (1979–85)

BOB McADOO

The team's biggest star in the Buffalo days was 6-foot-9 center/forward Bob McAdoo. The Braves selected him with the second overall pick in the 1972 NBA Draft. McAdoo had been a standout at the University of North Carolina. His impact with the Braves was immediate, as he won the NBA's Rookie of the Year Award in 1973.

In 1974, McAdoo captured the NBA's scoring title, his first of three straight titles. The next year, he was named the league's MVP. McAdoo was a true standout for Buffalo, which nevertheless traded him in December 1976 after a change in ownership. McAdoo went on to win NBA titles with the Lakers in 1982 and 1985. He entered the Basketball Hall of Fame in 2000.

TEAM STATS AND RECORDS

ALL-TIME RECORD

- **Regular season**: 1,706–2,408
- **Postseason**: 63–79

TOP COACHES

- **Mike Dunleavy** (2003–10); 215–326 (regular season); 7–5 (postseason)
- **Doc Rivers** (2013–20); 356–208 (regular season); 27–32 (postseason)

CAREER LEADERS

- **Games**: DeAndre Jordan, 750
- **Points**: Randy Smith, 12,735
- **Rebounds**: DeAndre Jordan, 7,988
- **Assists**: Chris Paul, 4,023
- **Steals**: Randy Smith, 1,072
- **Blocked shots**: DeAndre Jordan, 1,277

Sam Cassell, *left*, and Corey Maggette celebrate during the Clippers' win over the Denver Nuggets to clinch their 2006 playoff series.

GREATEST SEASONS

In the spring of 2006, the Clippers reminded fans that there are two NBA teams in Los Angeles. First they won 47 games to make the playoffs for the first time in nine years. Forward Elton Brand averaged 24.7 points and ten rebounds. Point guard Sam Cassell and forward Corey Maggette each scored more than 17 points per game. Seeded sixth in the Western Conference playoffs, the Clippers knocked off third-seeded Denver four games to one in the first round. That was the team's first playoff series victory since it moved from Buffalo. The

Elton Brand was a key player in the Clippers' first playoff series win in Los Angeles.

Clippers lost to the second-seeded Phoenix Suns in seven games in the conference semifinals. However, it was still a memorable year for fans of the "other" Los Angeles team.

TEAM HISTORY

The Minneapolis Lakers joined the BAA in 1948. Led by star center George Mikan, they won the league title that year. After the BAA became the NBA, Minneapolis won four of the first five NBA titles.

LeBron James shoots during a 2021 playoff game.

In 1960, the team's owner decided to head west. He moved the team to Los Angeles. The Lakers have been a power in the league ever since.

Behind coach John Kundla, *top*, and George Mikan (99), the Minneapolis Lakers became the NBA's first dynasty.

GREATEST PLAYERS

- **Kareem Abdul-Jabbar**, C (1975–89)
- **Elgin Baylor**, F (1958–71)
- **Kobe Bryant**, G (1996–2016)
- **Wilt Chamberlain**, C (1968–73)
- **Anthony Davis**, F (2019–)
- **Gail Goodrich**, G (1965–68, 1970–76)
- **LeBron James**, F (2018–)
- **Earvin "Magic" Johnson**, G (1979–91, 1995–96)
- **Slater Martin**, G (1949–56)
- **George Mikan**, C (1948–54, 1955–56)
- **Vern Mikkelsen**, F (1949–59)
- **Shaquille O'Neal**, C (1996–2004)
- **Jim Pollard**, F (1948–55)
- **Jerry West**, G (1960–74)
- **James Worthy**, F (1982–94)

TEAM STATS AND RECORDS

ALL-TIME RECORD

- **Regular season**: 3,427–2,331
- **Postseason**: 456–305; 17 NBA titles

TOP COACHES

- **John Kundla** (1948–59); 423–302 (regular season); 60–35, five NBA titles (postseason)
- **Pat Riley** (1981–90); 533–194 (regular season); 102–47, four NBA titles (postseason)
- **Phil Jackson** (1999–04, 2005–11); 610–292 (regular season); 118–63, five NBA titles (postseason)

CAREER LEADERS

- **Games**: Kobe Bryant, 1,346
- **Points**: Kobe Bryant, 33,643
- **Rebounds**: Elgin Baylor, 11,463
- **Assists**: Magic Johnson, 10,141
- **Steals**: Kobe Bryant, 1,944
- **Blocked shots**: Kareem Abdul-Jabbar, 2,694

COACH RILEY

Some of the finest coaches in NBA history have spent time with the Lakers. Among them was Pat Riley. The former NBA point guard became the Lakers' coach in 1981. He guided the team to championships in 1982, 1985, 1987, and 1988.

Riley later coached the New York Knicks for four seasons. He brought them into the NBA Finals in 1994. The next year, he became the coach for the Miami Heat. He helped the team win the title in 2006. Riley was named NBA Coach of the Year in 1990, 1993, and 1997.

Kobe Bryant, *left*, and Shaquille O'Neal led their team to three championships together.

GREATEST SEASONS

The Lakers have had many great eras. They were dominant in their Minneapolis years. Then they won three straight titles starting in 2000 with Shaquille O'Neal and Kobe Bryant. They won two more with Bryant leading the way in 2009 and 2010. But the version of the Lakers most fans remember best were the "Showtime" teams of the 1980s. Led by point guard Magic Johnson and center Kareem Abdul-Jabbar, every Lakers home game became an event. Celebrities and fans flocked to the Fabulous Forum to watch LA's fast-break offense. The Lakers won five NBA titles in the 1980s and made the NBA Finals three other times in the decade. Few teams can match that run of success.

TEAM HISTORY

The Vancouver Grizzlies joined the NBA in 1995. They came into the league the same year as the Toronto Raptors, making them the first two NBA teams to play in Canada. The Grizzlies struggled from the start. They never won more than 23 games in a season while playing in Vancouver. After six years, the team's owners moved them to Memphis, Tennessee. It was a city with a great college basketball scene. The fans loved the pro game too. By their third season in Memphis, the Grizzlies were a playoff team. They won their first playoff series in 2011. That began a string of seven straight playoff seasons.

GREATEST PLAYERS

- **Shareef Abdur-Rahim**, F (1996–2001)
- **Tony Allen**, G (2010–17)
- **Shane Battier**, F (2001–06, 2011)
- **Mike Bibby**, G (1998–2001)
- **Mike Conley**, G (2007–19)
- **Marc Gasol**, C (2008–19)
- **Pau Gasol**, F-C (2001–08)
- **Rudy Gay**, F (2006–13)
- **O. J. Mayo**, G (2008–12)
- **Mike Miller**, F (2003–08, 2013–14)
- **Ja Morant**, G (2019–)
- **Zach Randolph**, F (2009–17)
- **Bryant Reeves**, C (1995–2001)
- **Jonas Valančiūnas**, C (2018– 2021)
- **Jason Williams**, G (2001–05, 2011)

WHAT'S IN A NAME?

When the NBA added a basketball team to Vancouver, the team decided to call itself the Grizzlies. Grizzly bears are native to British Columbia, the Canadian province in which Vancouver is located. Some people wondered why the nickname didn't change when the team moved to Memphis. After all, there are no grizzly bears in Tennessee. But many fans still love their team's nickname.

Guard Ja Morant goes up for a shot in a 2021 playoff game against the Jazz.

TEAM STATS AND RECORDS

ALL-TIME RECORD

- **Regular season**: 864–1,201
- **Postseason**: 30–50

TOP COACHES

- **Lionel Hollins** (1999–2000, 2004, 2009–13); 214–201 (regular season); 18–17 (postseason)
- **Dave Joerger** (2013–16); 147–99 (regular season); 9–13 (postseason)

CAREER LEADERS

- **Games**: Mike Conley, 788
- **Points**: Mike Conley, 11,733
- **Rebounds**: Marc Gasol, 5,942
- **Assists**: Mike Conley, 4,509
- **Steals**: Mike Conley, 1,161
- **Blocked shots**: Marc Gasol, 1,135

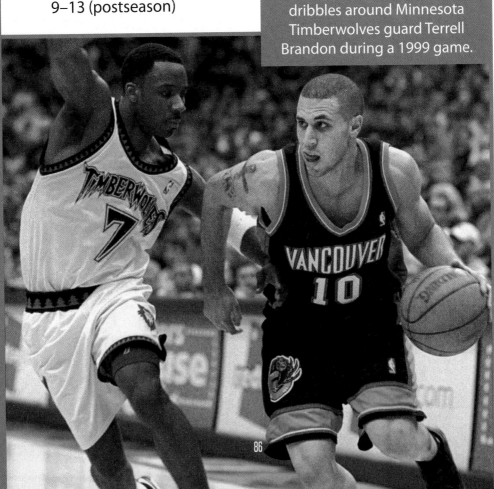

Grizzlies point guard Mike Bibby dribbles around Minnesota Timberwolves guard Terrell Brandon during a 1999 game.

GREATEST SEASONS

Going into the 2013 NBA playoffs, the Grizzlies had a score to settle. The previous season, the Los Angeles Clippers had knocked them out in seven games in the first round. The teams met again in the first round. After losing the first two games, the Grizzlies won four straight to take the series. In the second round, Memphis met top-seeded Oklahoma City. The Oklahoma City Thunder were heavily favored, especially after winning the first game. But then the Grizzlies took over. The Thunder had

In 2011, center Marc Gasol led the Grizzlies past the first round of the playoffs.

no answer for center Marc Gasol and forward Zach Randolph. The Grizzlies won the next four games to upset the Thunder. The run finally ended in the Western Conference finals when Memphis was swept by the second-seeded San Antonio Spurs. But the Grizzlies showed they could compete in the rugged Western Conference.

MIAMI HEAT

Jimmy Butler dunks against the Magic during a 2020 game.

TEAM HISTORY

The Heat joined the NBA in 1988. They had a rough start, winning just 33 games during their first two seasons. But soon they were a playoff power, reaching the conference finals in 1997. They won their first NBA title in 2006. That's when head coach Pat Riley, star guard Dwyane Wade, and legendary center Shaquille O'Neal led them past the Dallas Mavericks in the Finals. Four years later, they shook up the entire league when they signed LeBron James and Chris Bosh. This created the "super team" trend that emerged in the 2010s.

GREATEST PLAYERS

- **Bam Adebayo**, C (2017–)
- **Chris Bosh**, F (2010–16)
- **Jimmy Butler**, F-G (2019–)
- **Tim Hardaway**, G (1996–2001)
- **Udonis Haslem**, F-C (2003–)
- **LeBron James**, F (2010–14)
- **Eddie Jones**, G (2000–05, 2007)
- **Alonzo Mourning**, C (1995–2002, 2005–08)
- **Shaquille O'Neal**, C (2004–08)
- **Gary Payton**, G (2005–07)
- **Glen Rice**, F (1989–95)
- **Rony Seikaly**, C (1988–94)
- **Steve Smith**, G (1991–94, 2005)
- **Dwyane Wade**, G (2003–16, 2018–19)
- **Hassan Whiteside**, C (2014–19)

The Heat traded for powerful center Shaquille O'Neal in 2004 and immediately became championship contenders.

TEAM STATS AND RECORDS

Dwyane Wade set several team records during his 15 seasons with the Heat.

ALL-TIME RECORD

- **Regular season:** 1,378–1,261
- **Postseason:** 138–111; three NBA titles

TOP COACHES

- **Pat Riley** (1995–2003, 2005–08); 454–395 (regular season); 34–36, one NBA title (postseason)
- **Erik Spoelstra** (2008–); 607–424 (regular season); 85–58, two NBA titles (postseason)

CAREER LEADERS

- **Games:** Dwyane Wade, 948
- **Points:** Dwyane Wade, 21,556
- **Rebounds:** Udonis Haslem, 5,755
- **Assists:** Dwyane Wade, 5,310
- **Steals:** Dwyane Wade, 1,492
- **Blocked shots:** Alonzo Mourning, 1,625

THE DECISION

The Heat knew they needed to get some help for Dwyane Wade after the 2009–10 season. General manager Pat Riley signed Toronto Raptors All-Star forward Chris Bosh. Then the basketball world waited for free agent superstar LeBron James to decide where to play. Would he remain with his hometown Cavs or look for greener pastures elsewhere?

James kept teams and fans anxious by announcing he would make his choice on national TV on July 8, 2010. The one-hour special was simply called "The Decision." When James finally told the world where he was headed, Heat fans jumped for joy. James, Bosh, and Wade were greeted by fans at a lavish party at the team's arena. The trio led the Heat to the NBA Finals the next four years, winning twice.

Miami's Dwyane Wade, *left*, LeBron James, *right*, and Chris Bosh, *back*, celebrate after winning the 2013 NBA title.

GREATEST SEASONS

The trio of LeBron James, Dwyane Wade, and Chris Bosh was nearly unstoppable. In their four years together in Miami, the Heat won four division titles and four Eastern Conference titles. The Dallas Mavericks upset Miami in the 2011 NBA Finals. However, the Heat defeated the Oklahoma City Thunder and San Antonio Spurs in the Finals the next two years.

TEAM HISTORY

The Milwaukee Bucks entered the league in 1968. They had the worst record in the Eastern Division that year. That gave them a fifty-fifty chance to win the No. 1 draft pick in 1969. A coin flip gave the Bucks the pick. With that choice, Milwaukee selected center Kareem Abdul-Jabbar. Two years later, they won the NBA title. Abdul-Jabbar led them back to the Finals in 1974, but they lost to the Boston Celtics. That proved to be the last time they reached the Finals until 2021. That's when the team, led by star forward Giannis Antetokounmpo, won its second NBA title.

GREATEST PLAYERS

- **Kareem Abdul-Jabbar**, C (1969–75)
- **Ray Allen**, G (1996–2003)
- **Giannis Antetokounmpo**, F (2013–)
- **Andrew Bogut**, C (2005–12)
- **Junior Bridgeman**, F-G (1975–84, 1987)
- **Terry Cummings**, F (1984–89, 1995–96)
- **Bob Dandridge**, F (1969–77, 1981)
- **Brandon Jennings**, G (2009–13, 2018)
- **Marques Johnson**, F-G (1977–84)
- **Bob Lanier**, C (1980–84)
- **Jon McGlocklin**, G (1968–76)
- **Sidney Moncrief**, G (1979–89)
- **Michael Redd**, G (2000–11)
- **Oscar Robertson**, G (1970–74)
- **Glenn Robinson**, F (1994–2002)

The Bucks celebrate their 2021 championship after beating the Phoenix Suns in the NBA Finals.

93

TEAM STATS AND RECORDS

ALL-TIME RECORD
- **Regular season:** 2,231–2,048
- **Postseason:** 142–147; two NBA titles

TOP COACHES
- **Larry Costello** (1968–76); 410–264 (regular season); 37–23, one NBA title (postseason)
- **Don Nelson** (1976–87); 540–344 (regular season); 42–46 (postseason)

CAREER LEADERS
- **Games:** Junior Bridgeman, 711
- **Points:** Kareem Abdul-Jabbar, 14,211
- **Rebounds:** Kareem Abdul-Jabbar, 7,161
- **Assists:** Paul Pressey, 3,272
- **Steals:** Quinn Buckner, 1,042
- **Blocked shots:** Alton Lister, 804

Oscar Robertson drives to the hoop during a 1974 game.

BRANDON JENNINGS

Rookie Brandon Jennings scored 55 points in only his seventh NBA game. It was during Milwaukee's 129–125 victory over Golden State on November 14, 2009. That broke Abdul-Jabbar's team rookie record of 51 points. It also came within two points of matching Michael Redd's team record of 57. Warriors coach Don Nelson called Jennings's game "probably the best rookie performance I've ever witnessed in 30-some years of coaching."

GREATEST SEASONS

The 1970–71 Bucks faced high expectations. Led by head coach Larry Costello and second-year center Abdul-Jabbar, the Bucks were coming off an appearance in the Eastern Division finals in their second season. The addition of future Hall of Fame point guard Oscar Robertson made the difference. Robertson was past his prime after spending ten seasons with the Cincinnati Royals. But his experience was just what the young Bucks needed. Abdul-Jabbar led the league in scoring at 31.7 points per game. Robertson chipped in 19.4 points and 8.2 assists per game. Forward Bob Dandridge and guard Jon McGlocklin proved to be effective scorers as well. The Bucks won 66 games in the regular season—14 more than any other team in the league. Then they went 12–2 in the playoffs. They clinched the title with a four-game sweep of the Baltimore Bullets in the NBA Finals.

Bucks center Kareem Abdul-Jabbar goes up for a skyhook against the Bulls in November 1971.

Anthony Edwards dunks during a 2021 game against the Warriors.

TEAM HISTORY

The Minnesota Timberwolves joined the NBA in 1989. They were awful at first. But after six losing seasons, they started to build a winning team. They had an energetic, young head coach in Flip Saunders and a dynamic talent in forward Kevin Garnett. The Wolves made the playoffs for the first time in 1997. That was the first of eight straight playoff appearances. They were knocked out in the first round seven years in a row before putting together a run to the Western Conference finals in 2004. Minnesota then went 13 years without making the playoffs again.

GREATEST PLAYERS

- **Terrell Brandon**, G (1999–2002)
- **Sam Cassell**, G (2003–05)
- **Gorgui Dieng**, F-C (2013–20)
- **Anthony Edwards**, G (2020–)
- **Kevin Garnett**, F (1995–2007, 2015–16)
- **Tom Gugliotta**, F (1995–98)
- **Christian Laettner**, F (1992–96)
- **Kevin Love**, F (2008–14)
- **Stephon Marbury**, G (1996–99)
- **Sam Mitchell**, F (1989–92, 1995–2002)
- **Ricky Rubio**, G (2011–17, 2020–21)
- **Malik Sealy**, G-F (1999–2000)
- **Latrell Sprewell**, G-F (2003–05)
- **Wally Szczerbiak**, G-F (1999–2006)
- **Karl-Anthony Towns**, C (2015–)

Karl-Anthony Towns dunks against the Pelicans during a 2018 game.

TEAM STATS AND RECORDS

ALL-TIME RECORD
- **Regular season:** 1,003–1,545
- **Postseason:** 18–34

TOP COACHES
- **Flip Saunders** (1995–2005, 2014–15); 427–392 (regular season); 17–30 (postseason)
- **Tom Thibodeau** (2016–19); 97–107 (regular season); 1–4 (postseason)

CAREER LEADERS
- **Games:** Kevin Garnett, 970
- **Points:** Kevin Garnett, 19,201
- **Rebounds:** Kevin Garnett, 10,718
- **Assists:** Kevin Garnett, 4,216
- **Steals:** Kevin Garnett, 1,315
- **Blocked shots:** Kevin Garnett, 1,590

Kevin Garnett leaps for a shot during a 2004 playoff game.

Kevin Love grabs a rebound during a 2010 game.

GREATEST SEASONS

The 2003–04 Timberwolves were the best in the team's history. Garnett won the NBA MVP Award that year. Veterans Sam Cassell and Latrell Sprewell joined the team to help it finally win a playoff series. The Timberwolves beat the Denver Nuggets in five games. Then they held off the Sacramento Kings in seven games to reach the conference finals. However, with a berth to the Finals on the line, the Wolves lost to the Los Angeles Lakers in six games.

KG'S TRADE

By the 2007–08 season, the Wolves had missed the playoffs for three years in a row. They had also lost 50 games the previous season. Garnett was making more than $20 million per season. Because of that, the Wolves had a hard time signing other players to improve the team. Also, Garnett was upset that the team could not qualify for the playoffs. The Wolves finally traded him to the Celtics on July 31, 2007. They got five players and two first-round draft picks in return for Garnett. It was the largest package a team had ever received in a trade for one player. In 2015, Garnett went back to the Wolves and played with them for parts of two seasons before retiring.

TEAM HISTORY

New Orleans saw the NBA come and go with the Jazz, who played there in the late 1970s. They got a second chance in 2002 when the owners of the Charlotte Hornets moved the team to Louisiana. The city was devastated by Hurricane Katrina in 2005. The Hornets played most of the next two seasons in Oklahoma City, Oklahoma, while their arena was repaired. They came back to New Orleans full-time in 2007. In 2013, they changed their nickname to the Pelicans. In their first 19 seasons in New Orleans, they made the playoffs seven times and won two series.

CHANGING THE TEAM'S NAME

The owner of the New Orleans Hornets, Tom Benson, announced in 2013 that the team would change its nickname. He later said, "The pelican is a symbol for our city and region, and we're excited to start a new era in Louisiana basketball history." The name change came with a uniform change too. Instead of the Hornets' purple, teal, white, and gold colors, the Pelicans wore blue, red, and gold jerseys.

GREATEST PLAYERS

- **Ryan Anderson**, F (2012–16)
- **P. J. Brown**, F-C (2002–06)
- **Tyson Chandler**, C (2006–09)
- **Anthony Davis**, C (2012–19)
- **Baron Davis**, G (2002–05)
- **Tyreke Evans**, G-F (2013–17)
- **Jrue Holliday**, G (2013–20)
- **Brandon Ingram**, F (2019–)
- **Jamaal Magloire**, C (2002–05)
- **Emeka Okafor**, C (2009–12, 2018)
- **Chris Paul**, G (2005–11)
- **Peja Stojaković**, F (2006–10)
- **David West**, F (2003–11)
- **Zion Williamson**, F (2019–)

Zion Williamson dunks during a February 2021 game.

TEAM STATS AND RECORDS

ALL-TIME RECORD

- **Regular season**: 704–818
- **Postseason**: 20–29

TOP COACHES

- **Byron Scott** (2004–09); 203–216 (regular season); 8–9 (postseason)
- **Alvin Gentry** (2015–20); 175–225 (regular season); 5–4 (postseason)

CAREER LEADERS

- **Games**: David West, 530
- **Points**: Anthony Davis, 11,059
- **Rebounds**: Anthony Davis, 4,906
- **Assists**: Chris Paul, 4,228
- **Steals**: Chris Paul, 1,010
- **Blocked shots**: Anthony Davis, 1,121

Pelicans center Anthony Davis posts up against an Orlando Magic defender during a 2013 game.

GREATEST SEASONS

The Hornets' return to New Orleans in 2007 was a success in many ways. Not only did the community support the team, but the Hornets also won the Southwest Division title. They earned the second seed in the Western Conference playoffs and whipped the Dallas Mavericks four games to one in the first round. Point guard Chris Paul averaged 24.6 points and 12 assists during the series. The Hornets faced a veteran San Antonio Spurs team in the next round. The home team won each of the first six games before the Spurs took Game 7 on the road to knock out the Hornets.

New Orleans point guard Chris Paul led the Hornets to their first Southwest Division title in the 2007–08 season.

NEW YORK KNICKS

TEAM HISTORY

The New York Knickerbockers were founding members of the BAA in 1946. They joined the NBA in 1949 and have been playing at New York's Madison Square Garden ever since. They won two league titles in the early 1970s. They had another run of success after winning the 1984 NBA Draft lottery and selecting center

The Knicks' Julius Randle dunks during a playoff game in 2021 against the Hawks.

Patrick Ewing. With Ewing in the middle and guard John Starks making big plays, the Knicks reached the NBA Finals in 1994. They got back to the Finals five years later, but neither team could finish the job. The Knicks hit a rough stretch beginning in 2001, with just five playoff appearances and one series victory through 2021.

GREATEST PLAYERS

- **Carmelo Anthony**, F (2011–17)
- **Dick Barnett**, G (1965–73)
- **Dave DeBusschere**, F (1968–74)
- **Patrick Ewing**, C (1985–2000)
- **Walt Frazier**, G (1967–77)
- **Harry Gallatin**, F (1948–58)
- **Richie Guerin**, G (1956–63)
- **Allan Houston**, G (1996–2005)
- **Bernard King**, F (1982–1987)
- **Earl Monroe**, G (1971–80)
- **Charles Oakley**, F (1988–98)
- **Julius Randle**, F (2019–)
- **Willis Reed**, C-F (1964–74)
- **John Starks**, G (1990–98)
- **Amar'e Stoudemire**, C-F (2010–15)

BILL BRADLEY

Bill Bradley graduated from Princeton University in 1965 as a three-time basketball All-American. Bradley signed with the Knicks in 1967. A selfless passer and accurate shooter, the 6-foot-5 Bradley averaged 12.4 points per game in ten seasons, mostly as a small forward. He entered the Hall of Fame in 1983. He was a US senator from New Jersey from 1979 to 1997.

TEAM STATS AND RECORDS

ALL-TIME RECORD
- **Regular season:** 2,840–3,019
- **Postseason:** 187–193; two NBA titles

TOP COACHES
- **Joe Lapchick** (1947–56); 326–247 (regular season); 30–30 (postseason)
- **Red Holzman** (1967–77, 1978–82); 613–483 (regular season); 54–43, two NBA titles (postseason)

CAREER LEADERS
- **Games:** Patrick Ewing, 1,039
- **Points:** Patrick Ewing, 23,665
- **Rebounds:** Patrick Ewing, 10,759
- **Assists:** Walt Frazier, 4,791
- **Steals:** Patrick Ewing, 1,061
- **Blocked shots:** Patrick Ewing, 2,758

Carmelo Anthony grabs a rebound during a 2011 game in Madison Square Garden.

GREATEST SEASONS

The 1970 NBA Finals were a battle. The Knicks took on the Los Angeles Lakers. Much of the attention focused on the battle at center. The Lakers had the legendary Wilt Chamberlain. Meanwhile, New York's leading scorer and rebounder was Willis Reed, who won the NBA MVP Award that year.

The Knicks won three of the first five games. They had a chance to knock the Lakers out in Game 6. But Reed was injured and couldn't play. The Lakers won big to force Game 7 back in New York. Nobody knew whether Reed would be able to play. Then just before the game started, the Knicks captain hobbled through the tunnel and onto the court. Reed scored just four points in 27 minutes of action, but he held Chamberlain in check on defense. New York took a 113–99 victory and their first NBA title.

Walt Frazier, *right*, played a key role for the Knicks in the 1970 NBA Finals.

TEAM HISTORY

The Oklahoma City Thunder was founded in 1967 as the Seattle SuperSonics. The team was the first attempt at major league sports in Seattle, Washington. The Sonics were a big hit with their fans. They won the 1979 NBA title and were regular playoff participants. But eventually their owners wanted a new arena, and the city refused to pay for it. So the team moved to Oklahoma City. Once again, it was the first major league sports team in the market, and the newly named Thunder thrived. They reached the playoffs ten times in their first 13 years and made it to the NBA Finals in 2012.

GREATEST PLAYERS

- **Freddie Brown**, G (1971–84)
- **Kevin Durant**, F (2007–16)
- **Dale Ellis**, G (1986–91, 1997–99)
- **Serge Ibaka**, C (2009–16)
- **Dennis Johnson**, G (1976–80)
- **Shawn Kemp**, F-C (1989–97)
- **Rashard Lewis**, F (1999–2007)
- **Xavier McDaniel**, F (1985–90)
- **Nate McMillan**, G (1986–98)
- **Gary Payton**, G (1990–2003)
- **Detlef Schrempf**, F (1993–99)
- **Jack Sikma**, C-F (1977–86)
- **Slick Watts**, G (1973–78)
- **Russell Westbrook**, G (2008–19)
- **Gus Williams**, G (1977–84)

Shai Gilgeous-Alexander takes off down the court during a 2021 game against the Mavericks.

TEAM STATS AND RECORDS

ALL-TIME RECORD

- **Regular season:** 2,349–2,011
- **Postseason:** 164–167; one NBA title

TOP COACHES

- **Lenny Wilkens** (1969–72, 1977–85); 478–402 (regular season); 37–32, one NBA title (postseason)
- **George Karl** (1992–98); 384–150 (regular season); 40–40 (postseason)

CAREER LEADERS

- **Games:** Gary Payton, 999
- **Points:** Russell Westbrook, 18,859
- **Rebounds:** Jack Sikma, 7,729
- **Assists:** Gary Payton, 7,384
- **Steals:** Gary Payton, 2,107
- **Blocked shots:** Serge Ibaka, 1,300

Kevin Durant dunks the ball during a 2009 game against the Sacramento Kings.

GREATEST SEASONS

The 1978–79 Sonics won their first division title in team history. Center Jack Sikma and guards Gus Williams and Dennis Johnson led a balanced scoring attack. Seven players averaged at least 11 points per game. Seattle's talented lineup helped them beat the Los Angeles Lakers in the first round of the playoffs. Then they edged the Phoenix Suns in seven games to reach the NBA Finals. There, they knocked off the Washington Bullets in five games for the team's first league title.

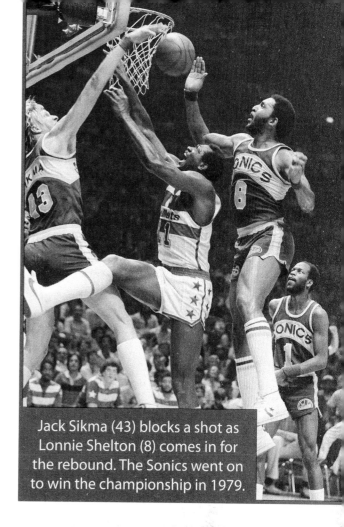

Jack Sikma (43) blocks a shot as Lonnie Shelton (8) comes in for the rebound. The Sonics went on to win the championship in 1979.

EARLY YEARS IN OKLAHOMA

The SuperSonics moved to Oklahoma City in 2008. The Thunder struggled through their first season but improved in 2009–10. They went 50–32 and made the playoffs. The Thunder faced the defending champions, the Los Angeles Lakers. Many people were excited to see the battle between the Thunder's up-and-coming Kevin Durant and the Lakers' superstar Kobe Bryant. The Thunder gave the Lakers a scare but were ultimately eliminated in six games.

Oklahoma City came back strong in 2010–11. They earned their first Northwest Division title and another berth in the playoffs. The Thunder eventually fell to the Dallas Mavericks, but it was hard for fans to be disappointed after such an exciting season.

ORLANDO MAGIC

TEAM HISTORY

The Orlando Magic joined the NBA in 1989. They built a winning team quickly, thanks in part to winning the 1992 NBA Draft lottery. That allowed them to select center Shaquille O'Neal. With Shaq leading the way, the Magic reached the NBA Finals in 1995 and the Eastern Conference finals the next year. O'Neal left after four years, and the team's playoff success left with him. Orlando did get back to the NBA Finals in 2009 with another young center, Dwight Howard, dominating inside.

Chasson Randle leaps for the basket during a 2021 game against the Philadelphia 76ers.

GREATEST PLAYERS

- **Nick Anderson**, G-F (1989–99)
- **Darrell Armstrong**, G (1995–2003)
- **Evan Fournier**, G-F (2014–21)
- **Horace Grant**, F (1994–99, 2001–02)
- **Anfernee Hardaway**, G (1993–99)
- **Grant Hill**, F (2000–07)
- **Dwight Howard**, C (2004–12)
- **Rashard Lewis**, F (2007–10)
- **Tracy McGrady**, G-F (2000–04)
- **Jameer Nelson**, G (2004–14)
- **Shaquille O'Neal**, C (1992–96)
- **Dennis Scott**, F (1990–97)
- **Scott Skiles**, G (1989–94)
- **Hedo Turkoglu**, F (2004–09, 2010–13)
- **Nikola Vučević**, C (2012–21)

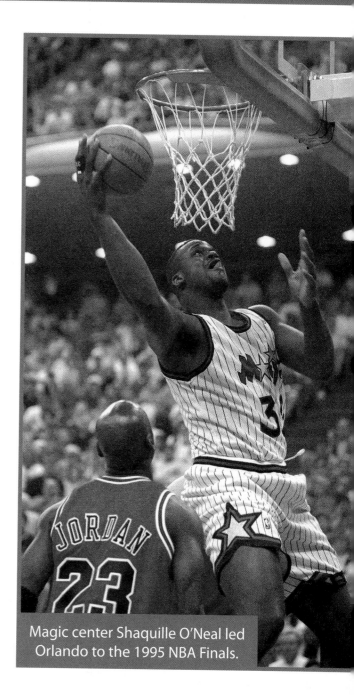

Magic center Shaquille O'Neal led Orlando to the 1995 NBA Finals.

TEAM STATS AND RECORDS

ALL-TIME RECORD

- **Regular season:** 1,212–1,345
- **Postseason:** 59–74

TOP COACHES

- **Brian Hill** (1993–97, 2005–07); 459–267 (regular season); 18–22 (postseason)
- **Stan Van Gundy** (2007–12); 259–135 (regular season); 31–28 (postseason)

CAREER LEADERS

- **Games:** Nick Anderson, 692
- **Points:** Dwight Howard, 11,435
- **Rebounds:** Dwight Howard, 8,072
- **Assists:** Jameer Nelson, 3,501
- **Steals:** Nick Anderson, 1,004
- **Blocked shots:** Dwight Howard, 1,344

GREATEST SEASONS

The 1994–95 Magic won 57 games, which was the most in the Eastern Conference. O'Neal led the NBA in scoring at 29.3 points per game. Guard Anfernee Hardaway chipped in 20.9 points and 7.2 assists per game. Forwards Horace Grant and Nick Anderson were key contributors. The Magic defeated the Boston Celtics in four games, the Chicago Bulls in six, and the Indiana Pacers in seven to reach the NBA Finals. Then they ran out of gas and were swept by the defending champions, the Houston Rockets.

SUPERMAN

In 2008, Dwight Howard created a buzz at All-Star weekend when he became the tallest player ever to win the Slam Dunk Contest. The 6-foot-11 Howard played up to his nickname, "Superman," by wearing a red cape with an S on the chest. He got a perfect score from the judges for his first two dunks. In the final round, both of his slams drew immense applause from the crowd. "I don't think people want to see the same old dunks. They want to see something else, see some spice," said Howard, who is known for his fun, joking personality.

The Magic's Nick Anderson dunks against the New Jersey Nets during a 1991 game.

TEAM HISTORY

The 76ers began play in 1949 as the Syracuse Nationals in New York. The Nats reached the NBA Finals in their first season and won the league title in 1955. Eventually the team's owner wanted a bigger market so the team could sell more tickets. He moved the team to Philadelphia. The team's name was changed to the Philadelphia 76ers, honoring the country's founding there in 1776. The 76ers have had some great teams and amazing players throughout their history. They won NBA titles in 1967 and 1983.

GREATEST PLAYERS

- **Charles Barkley**, F (1984–92)
- **Wilt Chamberlain**, C (1964–68)
- **Maurice Cheeks**, G (1978–89)
- **Doug Collins**, G (1973–81)
- **Billy Cunningham**, F (1965–72, 1974–76)
- **Joel Embiid**, C (2016–)
- **Julius Erving**, F (1976–87)
- **Hal Greer**, G-F (1958–73)
- **Andre Iguodala**, F (2004–12)
- **Allen Iverson**, G (1996–2006, 2009–10)
- **Bobby Jones**, F (1978–86)
- **Moses Malone**, C-F (1982–86, 1993–94)
- **Dolph Schayes**, F (1949–64)
- **Ben Simmons**, G (2017–)
- **Andrew Toney**, G (1980–88)

Joel Embiid looks to get around a Hawks player during a 2021 playoff game.

TEAM STATS AND RECORDS

ALL-TIME RECORD
- **Regular season**: 2,949–2,746
- **Postseason**: 235–224; three NBA titles

TOP COACHES
- **Al Cervi** (1949–57); 294–201 (regular season); 33–26, one NBA title (postseason)
- **Alex Hannum** (1960–63, 1966–68); 257–145 (regular season); 26–20, one NBA title (postseason)
- **Billy Cunningham** (1977–85); 454–196 (regular season); 66–39, one NBA title (postseason)

CAREER LEADERS
- **Games**: Hal Greer, 1,122
- **Points**: Hal Greer, 21,586
- **Rebounds**: Dolph Schayes, 11,256
- **Assists**: Maurice Cheeks, 6,212
- **Steals**: Maurice Cheeks, 1,942
- **Blocked shots**: Julius Erving, 1,293

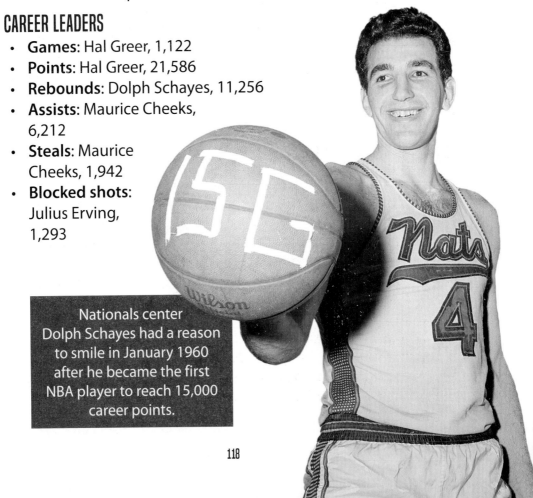

Nationals center Dolph Schayes had a reason to smile in January 1960 after he became the first NBA player to reach 15,000 career points.

GREATEST SEASONS

The 76ers played like a team on a mission in 1982–83. In the previous three seasons, they'd lost in the conference finals once and NBA Finals twice. Then they made a trade with the Houston Rockets to get two-time MVP Moses Malone. The veteran center averaged 24.5 points and 15.3 rebounds as the 76ers steamrolled the league, winning 65 games. Then they lost just one game in three playoff series. After having lost to the Lakers twice in the NBA Finals, they got sweet revenge with a four-game sweep to clinch the title.

Center Moses Malone takes a breather during a 1985 game.

TWENTY-FOUR SECONDS

One of the biggest changes in the history of basketball was the adoption of the shot clock. It establishes a number of seconds the offense has to shoot the ball, preventing teams from taking a big lead and then holding the ball to drain the game clock. The NBA implemented a 24-second shot clock in 1954. Syracuse Nationals owner Danny Biasone played a big role in making it happen. Biasone used simple math to determine the proper length of an NBA shot clock. He determined that in a well-paced game, each team attempted about 60 shots. Therefore, the total number of shots should be 120. In a 48-minute game, there are 2,880 seconds. Dividing 2,880 by 120 yields 24, and thus Biasone proposed a 24-second clock for teams to attempt a shot. The NBA adopted the shot clock and has kept it to this day.

PHOENIX SUNS

Guard Devin Booker goes for the ball during Game 5 of the 2021 NBA Finals.

TEAM HISTORY

The Phoenix Suns joined the NBA in 1968. They caught a bad break after losing a coin flip for the first pick in the 1969 draft. That pick turned out to be Hall of Fame center Kareem Abdul-Jabbar, who went to the Milwaukee Bucks. But that didn't set the Suns back for long. They reached the NBA Finals in 1976. The Suns were regular playoff participants for the next three decades. After a long dry stretch, they rebounded to post the second-best record in the league and reached the NBA Finals in 2020–21. However, they ultimately lost to the Bucks.

GREATEST PLAYERS

- **Alvan Adams**, F-C (1975–88)
- **Charles Barkley**, F (1992–96)
- **Devin Booker**, G (2015–)
- **Tom Chambers**, F (1988–93)
- **Walter Davis**, G (1977–88)
- **Connie Hawkins**, F (1969–73)
- **Jeff Hornacek**, G (1986–92)
- **Kevin Johnson**, G (1988–98, 2000)
- **Jason Kidd**, G (1996–2001)
- **Dan Majerle**, G (1988–1995, 2001–02)
- **Shawn Marion**, F (1999–2008)
- **Larry Nance**, F (1981–88)
- **Steve Nash**, G (1996–98, 2004–12)
- **Amar'e Stoudemire**, F (2002–10)
- **Dick Van Arsdale**, G-F (1968–77)
- **Paul Westphal**, G (1975–80, 1983–84)

THUNDER DAN

Dan Majerle originally earned the nickname "Thunder Dan" in his early days in the league. He was known for his rough inside play and thunderous dunks. Eventually Majerle became better known as a long-range shooting threat. He was the team's all-time leader in three-point field goals with 800 until Steve Nash broke his record in 2009. Majerle played seven seasons for the Suns. He also spent one year with the Cleveland Cavaliers and then played five seasons for the Miami Heat. He returned to Phoenix for the final year of his career. He retired as a Suns player before becoming an assistant coach for the team.

TEAM STATS AND RECORDS

ALL-TIME RECORD

- **Regular season:** 2,271–2,998
- **Postseason:** 147–149

TOP COACHES

- **Cotton Fitzsimmons** (1970–72, 1988–92, 1996); 341–208 (regular season); 22–22 (postseason)
- **John MacLeod** (1973–87); 579–543 (regular season); 37–44 (postseason)

CAREER LEADERS

- **Games:** Alvan Adams, 988
- **Points:** Walter Davis, 15,666
- **Rebounds:** Alvan Adams, 6,937
- **Assists:** Steve Nash, 6,997
- **Steals:** Alvan Adams, 1,289
- **Blocked shots:** Larry Nance, 940

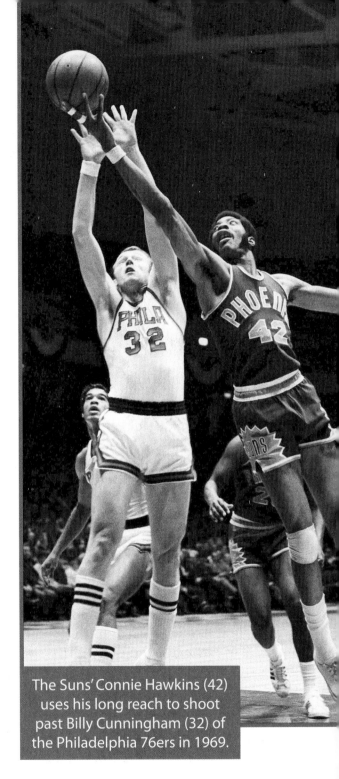

The Suns' Connie Hawkins (42) uses his long reach to shoot past Billy Cunningham (32) of the Philadelphia 76ers in 1969.

GREATEST SEASONS

The Suns set a team record with 62 wins in 1992–93. That gave them the best record in the NBA and set up an epic playoff run. Forward Charles Barkley averaged 25.6 points and 12.2 rebounds per game. Guards Kevin Johnson and Dan Majerle led an explosive offense.

The Suns were pushed to the brink in the first round of the playoffs. They lost the first two games of a best-of-five at home against the Lakers. But they rallied to win two games in Los Angeles and closed it out back at home in Game 5. Then they beat the San Antonio Spurs in six games, clinching the series with a two-point win on the road. Finally, they went the distance with the Seattle SuperSonics before winning the Western Conference

Dan Majerle, *right*, drives past the Bulls' Michael Jordan in Game 3 of the 1993 NBA Finals.

finals in seven games. That set up a meeting with the Chicago Bulls in the NBA Finals. Michael Jordan's team had won two straight league titles. The Bulls won the first two games of the series in Phoenix. But the Suns rallied to take two of three games in Chicago. However, in Game 6 a last-second three-pointer by Chicago's John Paxson gave the Bulls a one-point victory.

PORTLAND TRAIL BLAZERS

TEAM HISTORY

The Portland Trail Blazers entered the league in 1970. They struggled in their first six years. Then they caught fire and won the NBA title in their first playoff appearance in 1977. They've had several strong teams since, including the Clyde Drexler-led squad that reached the NBA Finals in 1990 and 1992.

GREATEST PLAYERS

- **LaMarcus Aldridge**, F (2006–15)
- **Clyde Drexler**, G (1983–95)
- **Kevin Duckworth**, C (1986–93)
- **Jerome Kersey**, F (1984–95)
- **Damian Lillard**, G (2012–)
- **Maurice Lucas**, F (1976–80)
- **CJ McCollum**, G (2013–)
- **Terry Porter**, G (1985–95)
- **Zach Randolph**, F (2001–07)
- **Cliff Robinson**, F (1989–97)
- **Brandon Roy**, G (2006–11)
- **Arvydas Sabonis**, C (1995–2001, 2002–03)
- **Mychal Thompson**, C-F (1978–86)
- **Rasheed Wallace**, F (1996–2004)
- **Buck Williams**, F (1989–96)

Portland's Terry Porter flies through the air between Phoenix Suns defenders to score early in a 1992 playoff game.

Damian Lillard shoots a three-pointer over Michael Porter Jr. of the Denver Nuggets in a 2021 game.

TEAM STATS AND RECORDS

ALL-TIME RECORD

- **Regular season:** 2,211–1,905
- **Postseason:** 119–155; one NBA title

TOP COACHES

- **Jack Ramsay** (1976–86); 453–367 (regular season); 29–30, one NBA title (postseason)
- **Terry Stotts** (2012–21); 402–318 (regular season); 22–40 (postseason)

CAREER LEADERS

- **Games:** Clyde Drexler, 867
- **Points:** Clyde Drexler, 18,040
- **Rebounds:** LaMarcus Aldridge, 5,434
- **Assists:** Terry Porter, 5,319
- **Steals:** Clyde Drexler, 1,795
- **Blocked shots:** Mychal Thompson, 768

GREATEST SEASONS

Center Bill Walton led the Trail Blazers to an unlikely NBA title in 1976–77. In addition to scoring 18.6 points per game, Walton posted a league-high 14.4 rebounds and 3.2 blocked shots per game that season. Bruising forward Maurice Lucas helped him dominate inside, averaging 20.2 points and 11.4 rebounds. Guard Lionel Hollins chipped in 14.7 points per game. The Blazers had never reached the playoffs, but they took to the postseason like veterans. They defeated the Chicago Bulls in the first round. Then they upset the second-seeded Denver Nuggets in six games to reach the Western Conference finals. A four-game sweep of the Los Angeles Lakers put them in the NBA Finals. They faced Julius Erving and the Philadelphia 76ers. Walton was a force again. He averaged 18.5 points and 19 rebounds to win the series MVP Award as the Blazers took the title in six games.

Maurice Lucas of the Trail Blazers helped his team win the NBA Finals in 1977.

BIG REDHEAD

One of the key players on the 1977 championship-winning Trail Blazers was center Bill Walton. Known as the "Big Redhead," Walton suffered through repeated foot and knee injuries, keeping him from becoming an even better player than he was. Walton entered the Basketball Hall of Fame in 1993.

SACRAMENTO KINGS

TEAM HISTORY

Few teams in any sport have bounced around more than the Kings. They began play as the Rochester Royals in Rochester, New York. They joined the NBL in 1945 before moving to the BAA for its final season in 1948–49. The Royals then joined the NBA, and in 1951 they won the league title. Due to financial struggles, the team moved to Cincinnati, Ohio, in 1957. The great Oscar Robertson starred for the Royals throughout the 1960s. However, the team never advanced further than the division finals. In 1972, the Royals were on the move again. The team was sold to a group from Missouri. The Royals became the Kings and split their first three years between Kansas City, Missouri, and Omaha, Nebraska. They eventually settled on Kansas City and stayed there until 1985, when they moved to Sacramento, California.

GREATEST PLAYERS

- **Nate Archibald**, G (1970–76)
- **Harrison Barnes**, F (2018–)
- **Mike Bibby**, G (2001–08)
- **Bob Davies**, G (1948–55)
- **Vlade Divac**, C (1999–2004)
- **Sam Lacey**, C (1970–81)
- **Jerry Lucas**, F (1963–69)
- **Mitch Richmond**, G (1991–98)
- **Arnie Risen**, C (1948–55)

- **Oscar Robertson**, G (1960–70)
- **Peja Stojaković**, F (1999–2006)
- **Maurice Stokes**, F-C (1955–58)
- **Jack Twyman**, F (1955–66)
- **Bobby Wanzer**, G (1948–57)
- **Chris Webber**, F (1998–2005)

Harrison Barnes (40) looks for an open teammate during a 2021 game.

TEAM STATS AND RECORDS

ALL-TIME RECORD

- **Regular season:** 2,624–3,135
- **Postseason:** 80–107; one NBA title

TOP COACHES

- **Les Harrison** (1948–55); 295–181 (regular season); 19–19, one NBA title (postseason)
- **Rick Adelman** (1999–2006); 395–229 (regular season); 34–35 (postseason)

CAREER LEADERS

- **Games:** Sam Lacey, 888
- **Points:** Oscar Robertson, 22,009
- **Rebounds:** Sam Lacey, 9,353
- **Assists:** Oscar Robertson, 7,731
- **Steals:** Sam Lacey, 950
- **Blocked shots:** Sam Lacey, 1,098

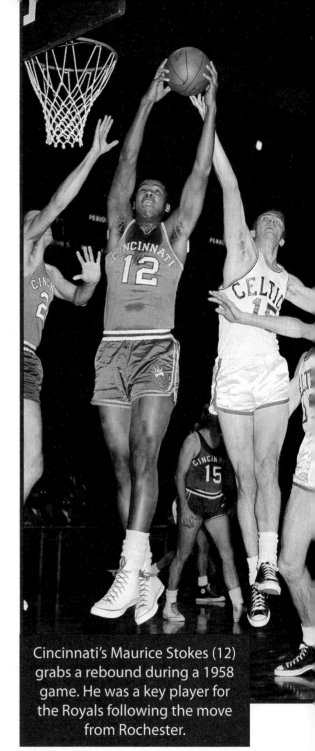

Cincinnati's Maurice Stokes (12) grabs a rebound during a 1958 game. He was a key player for the Royals following the move from Rochester.

GREATEST SEASONS

The Kings haven't had a lot of success, but they did win consecutive division titles in 2002 and 2003. Forwards Peja Stojaković and Chris Webber and guards Mike Bibby and Doug Christie led the way to three playoff series victories during those two years. The Kings reached the Western Conference finals in 2002 but lost a heartbreaking seven-game series to the Lakers.

The Royals' Oscar Robertson goes up for a shot during a 1970 game against the Chicago Bulls.

THE BIG O

Oscar Robertson, nicknamed the "Big O," was one of the best all-around players in NBA history. The 6-foot-5 guard could do it all, and his numbers back that up. After starring at the University of Cincinnati, Robertson began a Hall of Fame career with the city's NBA team in 1960.

Robertson led the NBA in assists seven times with the Royals. He also was the NBA scoring champion for the 1967–68 season, averaging 29.2 points per game. Robertson was traded to the Milwaukee Bucks after the 1969–70 season. During his ten seasons with the Royals, Robertson averaged a remarkable 29.3 points, 10.3 assists, and 8.5 rebounds per game.

TEAM HISTORY

The Spurs began play as the Dallas Chaparrals. They were founding members of the ABA in 1967. In 1973, they moved to San Antonio, Texas, and changed their name to the Spurs. They've been remarkably consistent, making the playoffs 47 times in their first 54 seasons. The Spurs didn't reach the NBA Finals until 1999, but then they went wild. They won five league titles in 16 years.

GREATEST PLAYERS

- **LaMarcus Aldridge**, C (2015–21)
- **Bruce Bowen**, F-G (2001–09)
- **DeMar DeRozan**, G-F (2018–21)
- **Tim Duncan**, F (1997–2016)
- **Sean Elliott**, F (1989–93, 1994–2001)
- **George Gervin**, F-G (1974–85)
- **Artis Gilmore**, C (1982–87)
- **Manu Ginóbili**, G (2002–18)
- **Avery Johnson**, G (1991–92, 1992–93, 1994–2001)
- **Larry Kenon**, F (1975–80)
- **Kawhi Leonard**, F (2011–18)
- **Tony Parker**, G (2001–18)
- **Alvin Robertson**, G (1984–89)
- **David Robinson**, C (1989–2003)
- **James Silas**, G (1972–81)

GEORGE GERVIN

George Gervin was one of the best pure scorers in NBA history. He went into the Basketball Hall of Fame in 1996. He was also named to the NBA 50th Anniversary All-Time Team. Gervin averaged 26.2 points per game in the NBA.

Keldon Johnson of the Spurs leaps to the basket during a 2021 game against the Suns.

TEAM STATS AND RECORDS

ALL-TIME RECORD

- **Regular season:** 2,605–1,760
- **Postseason:** 222–181; five NBA titles

TOP COACHES

- **Doug Moe** (1976–80); 177–135 (regular season); 9–13 (postseason)
- **Gregg Popovich** (1996–); 1,310–653 (regular season); 170–114, five NBA titles (postseason)

CAREER LEADERS

- **Games:** Tim Duncan, 1,392
- **Points:** Tim Duncan, 26,496
- **Rebounds:** Tim Duncan, 15,091
- **Assists:** Tony Parker, 6,829
- **Steals:** Manu Ginóbili, 1,392
- **Blocked shots:** Tim Duncan, 3,020

George Gervin, *right*, passes the ball in an April 1974 game against the Indiana Pacers.

Tony Parker drives to the hoop during a November 2005 game against the Boston Celtics.

GREATEST SEASONS

The Spurs' "Big Three" of Tim Duncan, Tony Parker, and Manu Ginóbili have earned plenty of accolades. The trio played together for 14 seasons and won four NBA titles. But Duncan also has a fifth ring. He helped the Spurs win the title in 1999, his second season in the league. Duncan teamed with center David Robinson to form a powerful front line. Behind the "Twin Towers," the Spurs tied for the division title and then rolled through the playoffs, losing just two games in four series.

TEAM HISTORY

The Toronto Raptors joined the league along with the Vancouver Grizzlies as the NBA expanded to Canada in 1995. The Grizzlies struggled to establish themselves and eventually moved. But the Raptors thrived in Canada's largest city. While they haven't had a lot of postseason success, they did make a memorable playoff run to win the NBA title in 2019.

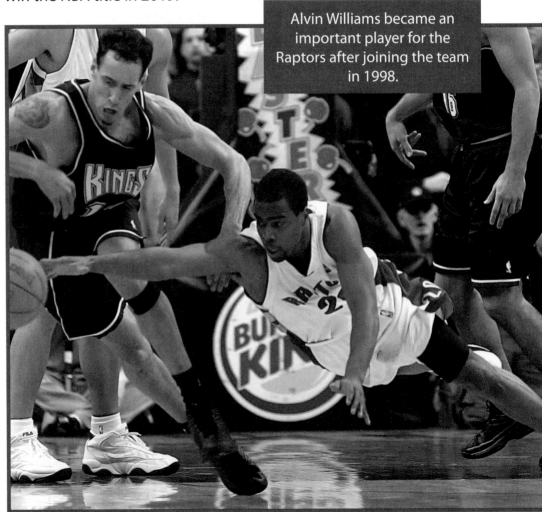

Alvin Williams became an important player for the Raptors after joining the team in 1998.

Vince Carter throws down a dunk during a 2003 game.

GREATEST PLAYERS

- **Andrea Bargnani**, F-C (2006–13)
- **Chris Bosh**, F-C (2003–10)
- **José Calderón**, G (2005–13)
- **Vince Carter**, G-F (1999–2004)
- **Antonio Davis**, F-C (1999–2003, 2006)
- **DeMar DeRozan**, G (2009–18)
- **Amir Johnson**, F (2009–15)
- **Kawhi Leonard**, F (2018–19)
- **Kyle Lowry**, G (2012–21)
- **Tracy McGrady**, F (1997–2000)
- **Morris Peterson**, G (2000–07)
- **Pascal Siakam**, F (2016–)
- **Jonas Valančiūnas**, C (2012–19)
- **Alvin Williams**, G (1998–2006)

CHRIS BOSH

Raptors fans had high expectations when the team selected Chris Bosh fourth in the 2003 draft. The 6-foot-11 forward had starred at Georgia Tech. He showcased his speed and talent immediately with the Raptors, quickly becoming a popular player. Bosh also engaged fans. He once made a funny video in which he pretended to be a cowboy. He posted it online because he wanted fans to vote him to the 2008 All-Star team. He ended up playing in that game as part of a string of 11 consecutive All-Star Game appearances, although some came after he left Toronto for the Miami Heat.

Chris Bosh became a superstar for the Raptors before leaving for the Miami Heat in 2010.

TEAM STATS AND RECORDS

ALL-TIME RECORD

- **Regular season:** 982–1,082
- **Postseason:** 55–62; one NBA title

TOP COACHES

- **Sam Mitchell** (2004–08); 156–189 (regular season); 3–8 (postseason)
- **Dwane Casey** (2011–18); 320–238 (regular season); 21–30 (postseason)
- **Nick Nurse** (2018–); 138–88 (regular season); 23–12, one NBA title (postseason)

CAREER LEADERS

- **Games:** DeMar DeRozan, 675
- **Points:** DeMar DeRozan, 13,296
- **Rebounds:** Chris Bosh, 4,776
- **Assists:** Kyle Lowry, 4,277
- **Steals:** Kyle Lowry, 873
- **Blocked shots:** Chris Bosh, 600

The Raptors celebrate their hard-won 2019 NBA title.

GREATEST SEASONS

The Raptors set the stage for their 2019 title when they made a trade for small forward Kawhi Leonard the previous summer. Leonard was a two-time NBA Defensive Player of the Year. He also won the 2014 NBA Finals MVP Award with the San Antonio Spurs. Leonard had just one year left on his contract, and he made it count. Leonard averaged 26.6 points per game while center Pascal Siakam averaged 16.9 points and 6.9 rebounds to lead the Raptors to the second-best record in the East. Leonard hit the biggest shot in franchise history, a buzzer-beater from the baseline, to lift Toronto over Philadelphia in Game 7 of the Eastern Conference semifinals. The Raptors rode that momentum to a six-game win over the Milwaukee Bucks to reach the NBA Finals. Leonard averaged 28.5 points and 9.8 rebounds in six games. The Raptors defeated the two-time defending champion, the Golden State Warriors, to win their first title.

TEAM HISTORY

It may seem strange to have a team named the Jazz playing in Utah, since the state isn't known for that type of music. New Orleans, however, is the birthplace of jazz. That's where this team was first founded in 1974. It spent five losing seasons in Louisiana. In 1979, the owners decided to move the team to Salt Lake City, Utah, which had been a strong market for the ABA's Utah Stars. It took five more years, but the Jazz became winners in Utah. They made the playoffs in 1984, starting a 20-year streak of reaching the postseason. That success continued as they entered the 2020–21 season, having made the playoffs for five straight seasons.

GREATEST PLAYERS

- **Thurl Bailey**, F-C (1983–91, 1999)
- **Carlos Boozer**, F (2004–10)
- **Adrian Dantley**, F-G (1979–86)
- **Mark Eaton**, C (1982–93)
- **Rudy Gobert**, C (2013–)
- **Darrell Griffith**, G (1980–91)
- **Gordon Hayward**, F (2010–17)
- **Jeff Hornacek**, G (1993–2000)
- **Andrei Kirilenko**, F (2001–11)
- **Karl Malone**, F (1985–2003)
- **Pete Maravich**, G (1974–80)
- **Paul Millsap**, F (2006–13)
- **Donovan Mitchell**, G (2017–)
- **John Stockton**, G (1984–2003)
- **Deron Williams**, G (2005–11)

Guard Donovan Mitchell, *center*, makes a pass while under pressure in a June 2021 game.

TEAM STATS AND RECORDS

ALL-TIME RECORD

- **Regular season:** 2,060–1,726
- **Postseason:** 133–153

TOP COACHES

- **Jerry Sloan** (1988–2011); 1,127–682 (regular season); 96–100 (postseason)
- **Quin Snyder** (2014–); 323–231 (regular season); 19–23 (postseason)

CAREER LEADERS

- **Games:** John Stockton, 1,504
- **Points:** Karl Malone, 36,374
- **Rebounds:** Karl Malone, 14,601
- **Assists:** John Stockton, 15,806
- **Steals:** John Stockton, 3,265
- **Blocked shots:** Mark Eaton, 3,064

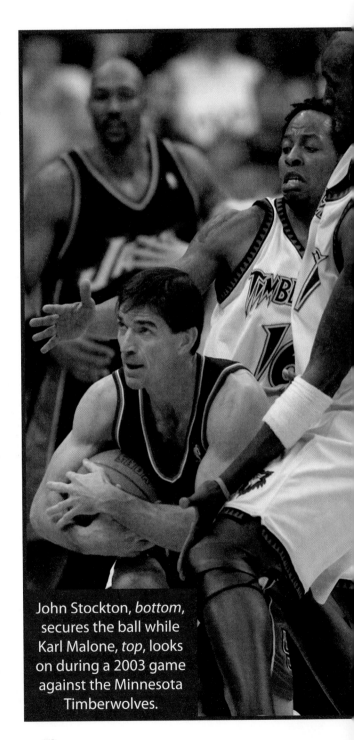

John Stockton, *bottom*, secures the ball while Karl Malone, *top*, looks on during a 2003 game against the Minnesota Timberwolves.

GREATEST SEASONS

The Jazz reached the NBA Finals in 1997 and 1998. Each year, they won more than 60 games and finished with the best record in the Western Conference. The Hall of Fame combo of point guard John Stockton and power forward Karl Malone was unstoppable. Guard Jeff Hornacek and forward Bryon Russell provided secondary scoring. But the Jazz had the misfortune of facing the Chicago Bulls in the NBA Finals both years. Utah made the Bulls work for their wins. Both years ended with Utah losing in six games, leaving the Jazz still looking for their first title.

Coach Jerry Sloan was the third cornerstone, along with John Stockton and Karl Malone, during the Jazz's run of success in the 1990s.

AWESOME DUO

John Stockton and Karl Malone had instant chemistry on the court when they became teammates. During their 18 years together, a huge percentage of Malone's points came from Stockton's assists. With Hall of Famer Jerry Sloan as their coach, Stockton and Malone made the pick-and-roll a lethal part of their game. A pick-and-roll is a designed play where one player sets a pick for another. Then he rolls to an open spot on the floor and looks for a pass from the other player so he can score a basket. Malone and Stockton worked it to perfection for nearly two decades.

TEAM HISTORY

The Wizards have had quite a few identities over the years. They were founded in 1961 as the Chicago Packers. They won just 18 games and changed their name to the Chicago Zephyrs the next year. The Zephyrs fared little better, and the team moved east to become the Baltimore Bullets in 1963. The team had much more success in Maryland. The Bullets even reached the NBA Finals in 1971. In 1973, they moved to Landover, Maryland, a suburb of Washington, DC. During their first year in Landover, they were known as the Capital Bullets. Then they adopted Washington as the team name. In 1997, the team moved to Washington, DC, and ditched the Bullets nickname, becoming the Washington Wizards.

Bradley Beal (3) tries to sneak past Ben Simmons of the 76ers during a 2021 playoff game.

Wizards guard John Wall dribbles the ball up the court against the Milwaukee Bucks in February 2011.

GREATEST PLAYERS

- **Gilbert Arenas**, G (2003–10)
- **Greg Ballard**, F (1977–85)
- **Bradley Beal**, G (2012–)
- **Walt Bellamy**, C (1961–65)
- **Phil Chenier**, G (1971–79)
- **Elvin Hayes**, F-C (1972–81)
- **Antawn Jamison**, F (2004–10)
- **Gus Johnson**, F-C (1963–72)
- **Michael Jordan**, G (2001–03)
- **Kevin Loughery**, G (1963–71)
- **Jeff Malone**, G (1983–90)
- **Jeff Ruland**, C-F (1981–86)
- **Wes Unseld**, C-F (1968–81)
- **John Wall**, G (2010–19)
- **Chris Webber**, F-C (1994–98)

ELVIN HAYES

Elvin Hayes was known as the "Big E." He was a big-time player in the NBA. Hayes played 16 seasons in the league from 1968 to 1984. He played for the Bullets from 1972 to 1981. His favorite move on offense was a turnaround jump shot. He would use it to get shots off against anyone, even taller players he faced either at forward or center. Hayes retired as the third all-time scorer in league history with 27,313 points and the third all-time leading rebounder at 16,279. Hayes was named to the Basketball Hall of Fame in 1990.

TEAM STATS AND RECORDS

ALL-TIME RECORD

- **Regular season:** 2,187–2,654
- **Postseason:** 99–138; one NBA title

TOP COACHES

- **Gene Shue** (1966–73, 1980–86); 522–505 (regular season); 19–36 (postseason)
- **Dick Motta** (1976–80); 185–143 (regular season); 27–24, one NBA title (postseason)
- **Wes Unseld** (1988–94); 202–345 (regular season); 2–3 (postseason)

CAREER LEADERS

- **Games:** Wes Unseld, 984
- **Points:** Elvin Hayes, 15,551
- **Rebounds:** Wes Unseld, 13,769
- **Assists:** John Wall, 5,282
- **Steals:** John Wall, 976
- **Blocked shots:** Elvin Hayes, 1,558

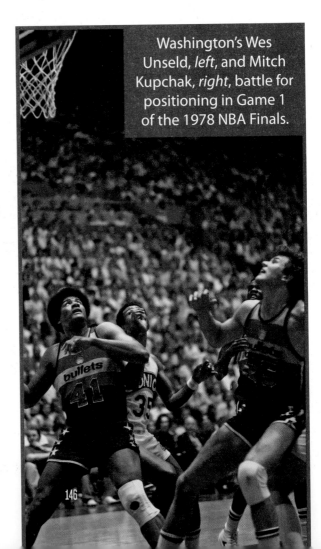

Washington's Wes Unseld, *left*, and Mitch Kupchak, *right*, battle for positioning in Game 1 of the 1978 NBA Finals.

GREATEST SEASONS

The Bullets had reached the NBA Finals in 1971 and 1975 and were swept both times. So when the team fought their way through the Eastern Conference playoffs in 1978, fans hoped for a better result against the Seattle SuperSonics in the Finals. And that's just what they got. Their veteran front line of center Wes Unseld and forwards Elvin Hayes and Bob Dandridge led the way as the Bullets won Game 7 105–99 to claim their first title.

Washington Bullets star Elvin Hayes admires the championship trophy his team won by defeating the Seattle SuperSonics in the 1978 NBA Finals.

KAREEM ABDUL-JABBAR c

Milwaukee Bucks (1969–75), Los Angeles Lakers (1975–89)

Kareem Abdul-Jabbar was the first pick of the 1969 NBA Draft. The Milwaukee Bucks center used his unstoppable skyhook shot to dominate opponents. Abdul-Jabbar retired as the NBA career leader in nine statistical categories. He remained the league's all-time leading scorer through 2021. But he wasn't just a compiler of stats—Abdul-Jabbar was a winner. He led the Bucks to the NBA title in his second season. He also won five titles with the Lakers in the 1980s.

Kareem Abdul-Jabbar

Games: 1,560
Points: 38,387
PPG: 24.6
Rebounds: 17,440
RPG: 11.2
Assists: 5,660
APG: 3.6
Blocked shots: 3,189
Steals: 1,160
Awards: NBA Rookie of the Year (1970), NBA MVP (1971, 1972, 1974, 1976, 1977, 1980), NBA Finals MVP (1971, 1985), 19 All-Star Games, First-Team All-NBA (1971–74, 1976, 1977, 1980, 1981, 1984, 1986)

Note: Steals and blocked shots were not tracked as official statistics until the 1973–74 season. Rebounds were not tracked as an official statistic until the 1950–51 season.

Ray Allen

RAY ALLEN G

Milwaukee Bucks (1996–2003),
Seattle SuperSonics (2003–07),
Boston Celtics (2007–12), Miami
Heat (2012–14)

Games: 1,300
Points: 24,505
PPG: 18.9
Three-pointers: 2,973
Three-pointers per game: 2.3
Rebounds: 5,272
RPG: 4.1
Assists: 4,361
Steals: 1,451
Awards: Ten All-Star Games

Ray Allen was one of the most accurate shooters in NBA history. He led the league in three-pointers three times and retired as the NBA's all-time three-point leader. Allen put up big numbers as the go-to scorer for the Bucks and Sonics in his prime. He later became more of a specialist, contributing key outside shooting for NBA championship teams in Boston and Miami. He might be best known for his game-tying three-pointer with five seconds left in Game 6 of the 2013 NBA Finals.

GIANNIS ANTETOKOUNMPO F

Milwaukee Bucks (2013–)

Giannis Antetokounmpo was born in Athens, Greece. He improved his scoring and rebounding averages in each of his first seven seasons, peaking at 29.5 points and 13.6 boards per game in 2019–20, when he won his first NBA MVP Award. Equally skilled at three-point shooting and running the floor, Antetokounmpo fills highlight reels with his monster slam dunks. But he's also one of the top all-around players in the game.

Giannis Antetokounmpo

Games: 589　**Assists:** 2,632
Points: 12,319　**APG:** 4.5
PPG: 20.9　**Blocked**
Rebounds: 5,371　**shots:** 765
RPG: 9.1　**Steals:** 692
Awards: NBA MVP (2019, 2020), NBA Finals MVP (2021), NBA Defensive Player of Year (2020), five All-Star Games, First-Team All-NBA (2019, 2020, 2021)

CHARLES BARKLEY F

Philadelphia 76ers (1984–92), Phoenix Suns (1992–96), Houston Rockets (1996–2000)

Charles Barkley was tireless in his pursuit of rebounds. Generously listed at 6-foot-6, Barkley finished in the top ten in rebounds per game nine times. He led the league in offensive rebounds three times. He went on to become a television broadcaster, where his frank commentary has made him a fan favorite.

Games: 1,073
Points: 23,757
PPG: 22.1
Rebounds: 12,546
RPG: 11.7
Assists: 4,215
APG: 3.9
Blocked shots: 888
Steals: 1,648
Awards: NBA MVP (1993), 11 All-Star Games, First-Team All-NBA (1988–91, 1993)

RICK BARRY F

*San Francisco Warriors (1965–67),
Oakland Oaks [ABA] (1968–69),
Washington Capitols [ABA] (1969–70),
New York Nets [ABA] (1970–72), Golden
State Warriors (1972–78), Houston
Rockets (1978–80)*

Rick Barry used his competitiveness
and talent to light up the scoreboard
for 14 seasons in the NBA and ABA.
Barry could beat players from the
outside. He could also slash to the
basket for a layup. And if he got
fouled, it was usually an automatic
two points. Barry used his unique
underhanded foul shot to lead the
league in free-throw percentage
seven times. He was
also one of the
first NBA stars
to jump to
the ABA and
lend credibility
to the
upstart league.

Rick Barry

Games: 1,020
Points: 25,279
PPG: 24.8
Rebounds: 6,863
RPG: 6.7
Assists: 4,952
APG: 4.9
Awards: NBA Rookie
of the Year (1966), NBA
Finals MVP (1975),
12 All-Star Games,
First-Team All-NBA
(1966, 1967, 1974–76),
First-Team All-ABA
(1969–72)

Charles Barkley

ELGIN BAYLOR F

Minneapolis Lakers (1958–60), Los Angeles Lakers (1960–71)

Elgin Baylor helped transform basketball from a game played on the ground to one played above the rim. His quickness and leaping ability helped him take over games by dominating close to the basket. Baylor and teammate Jerry West helped the Lakers establish themselves as the top team in the West after they moved to California. In his first three seasons in Los Angeles, Baylor averaged 35.3 points and 17.3 rebounds per game. With him on their team, the Lakers made the NBA Finals eight times.

Elgin Baylor

Games: 846　**RPG:** 13.5
Points: 23,149　**Assists:** 3,650
PPG: 27.4　**APG:** 4.3
Rebounds: 11,463
Awards: NBA Rookie of the Year (1959), 11 All-Star Games, First-Team All-NBA (1959–65, 1967–69)

LARRY BIRD F

Boston Celtics (1979–92)

Larry Bird was able to create shots for teammates with his vision and court sense. Bird was a threat to score from anywhere on the court, but he was especially accurate from a long distance. He helped the Celtics win three NBA titles in the 1980s. Bird was also part of the US "Dream Team" that won the gold medal at the 1992 Olympics.

Games: 897　**Assists:** 5,695
Points: 21,791　**APG:** 6.3
PPG: 24.3　**Blocked**
Rebounds: 8,974　**shots:** 755
RPG: 10　**Steals:** 1,556
Awards: NBA Rookie of the Year (1980), NBA MVP (1984–86), NBA Finals MVP (1984, 1986), 12 All-Star Games, First-Team All-NBA (1980–88)

Larry Bird

KOBE BRYANT G

Los Angeles Lakers (1996–2016)

Kobe Bryant began his Lakers career as a sidekick to Shaquille O'Neal. Together, the two of them won three straight NBA titles. Eventually Bryant's leadership skills caught up with his shooting and passing abilities. He led the Lakers to two more titles once he stepped out of O'Neal's shadow. He also remained an effective scorer throughout his career. Bryant poured in 60 points in his final game as a Laker.

Games: 1,346
Points: 33,643
PPG: 25
Rebounds: 7,047
RPG: 5.2
Assists: 6,306
APG: 4.7
Blocked shots: 640
Steals: 1,944
Awards: NBA MVP (2008), NBA Finals MVP (2009, 2010), 18 All-Star Games, First-Team All-NBA (2002–04, 2006–13)

Kobe Bryant

153

WILT CHAMBERLAIN c

Philadelphia Warriors (1959–62),
San Francisco Warriors (1962–65),
Philadelphia 76ers (1965–68),
Los Angeles Lakers (1968–73)

Wilt Chamberlain

Few players impacted the game the way Wilt Chamberlain did. The 7-footer towered over most of his opponents, but he was more than just a big man. He was a skilled and tireless competitor who rarely missed games and often played all 48 minutes

Games: 1,045   **RPG:** 22.9
Points: 31,419   **Assists:** 4,643
PPG: 30.1   **APG:** 4.4
Rebounds: 23,924
Awards: NBA Rookie of the Year (1960), NBA MVP (1960, 1966–68), NBA Finals MVP (1972), 13 All-Star Games, First-Team All-NBA (1960–62, 1964, 1966–68)

without a break. He was a prolific scorer who averaged a record 50.4 points in 1961–62. That was the season when he shattered the single-game scoring mark with 100 points in a game against the New York Knicks. He also holds the NBA career records for total rebounds and rebounds per game.

Bob Cousy (14)

BOB COUSY G

Boston Celtics (1950–63), Cincinnati Royals (1969–70)

Bob Cousy's dribbling skills were legendary and made him a fan favorite in the NBA's early days. Along with his elite ball-handling abilities, Cousy was one of the best passers of his generation. He led the NBA in assists for eight straight seasons.

Games: 924	**RPG:** 5.2
Points: 16,960	**Assists:** 6,955
PPG: 18.4	**APG:** 7.5
Rebounds: 4,786	
Awards: NBA MVP (1957), 13 All-Star Games, First-Team All-NBA (1952–61)	

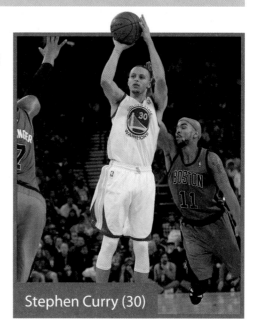

Stephen Curry (30)

STEPHEN CURRY G

Golden State Warriors (2009–)

The NBA has seen some great shooters over the years. But few have launched shots with the volume and accuracy of Stephen Curry. The son of former NBA sharpshooter Dell Curry has pushed the boundaries of what's considered "in shooting range." If Curry has the ball across the half-court line, he's in range. Curry had four of the five top single-season three-point totals in NBA history through 2021.

Games: 762	**Rebounds:** 3,503
Points: 18,434	**RPG:** 4.6
PPG: 24.2	**Assists:** 4,984
Three-pointers: 2,832	**APG:** 6.5
	Steals: 1,282
Three-pointers per game: 3.7	
Awards: NBA MVP (2015, 2016), seven All-Star Games, First-Team All-NBA (2015, 2016, 2019, 2021)	

Tim Duncan

TIM DUNCAN F

*San Antonio Spurs
(1997–2016)*

Tim Duncan grew up in the US Virgin Islands. He wanted to be an Olympic swimmer, but he ended up getting a basketball scholarship to Wake Forest University instead. Swimming's loss was the NBA's gain. Duncan became one of the most polished and productive players in the game's history. Duncan was a key figure in San Antonio's dynasty. He helped the Spurs win five NBA titles.

Games: 1,392
Points: 26,496
PPG: 19.0
Rebounds: 15,091
RPG: 10.8
Assists: 4,225
APG: 3.0
Blocked shots: 3,020
Steals: 1,025
Awards: NBA Rookie of the Year (1998), NBA MVP (2002, 2003), NBA Finals MVP (1999, 2003, 2005), 15 All-Star Games, First-Team All-NBA (1998–2005, 2007, 2013)

KEVIN DURANT F

Seattle SuperSonics (2007–08), Oklahoma City Thunder (2008–16), Golden State Warriors (2016–19), Brooklyn Nets (2020–)

Most defenders are either too small or too slow to match up with Kevin Durant. He's used that unique skill set to his advantage, winning four NBA scoring titles by age 25. He also helped Golden State win back-to-back titles.

Games: 884
Points: 23,883
PPG: 27.0
Rebounds: 6,239
RPG: 7.1
Assists: 3,681
APG: 4.2
Blocked shots: 986
Steals: 973
Awards: NBA Rookie of the Year (2008), NBA MVP (2014), NBA Finals MVP (2017, 2018), 11 All-Star Games, First-Team All-NBA (2010–14, 2018)

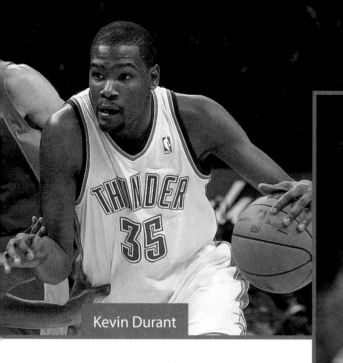
Kevin Durant

Julius Erving

JULIUS ERVING F

Virginia Squires [ABA] (1971–73),
New York Nets [ABA] (1973–76),
Philadelphia 76ers (1976–87)

Julius Erving was one of the greatest dunkers in the history of the sport. He was also a tenacious defender, an instinctive scorer, and an ambassador for the game. Fans flocked to arenas around the country to watch him play. Blessed with superior leaping ability and body control, Erving could bring down the house with a powerful dunk or a graceful finger-roll layup. He won three ABA scoring titles and two ABA championships. Then he helped the Philadelphia 76ers spend a decade as one of the NBA's best teams.

Games: 1,243   **Assists:** 5,176
Points: 30,026   **APG:** 4.2
PPG: 24.2   **Blocked**
Rebounds: **shots:** 1,941
10,525   **Steals:** 2,272
RPG: 8.5
Awards: ABA MVP (1974–76), ABA Playoffs MVP (1974, 1976), NBA MVP (1981), 16 All-Star Games, First-Team All-ABA (1973–76), First-Team All-NBA (1978, 1980–83)

PATRICK EWING c

New York Knicks (1985–2000),
Seattle SuperSonics (2000–01),
Orlando Magic (2001–02)

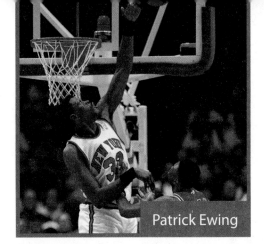

Patrick Ewing

Patrick Ewing was the No. 1 pick in the 1985 draft. He immediately helped turn the Knicks into contenders with his intimidating defense and shot-blocking abilities. He quickly polished his offensive game as well, averaging 20 points as a rookie and then topping that mark in each of the next 12 seasons. Ewing won two Olympic gold medals with Team USA.

Games: 1,183 **Assists:** 2,215
Points: 24,815 **APG:** 1.9
PPG: 21 **Blocked**
Rebounds: **shots:** 2,894
11,607 **Steals:** 1,136
RPG: 9.8
Awards: NBA Rookie of the Year (1986), 11 All-Star Games, First-Team All-NBA (1990)

WALT FRAZIER g

New York Knicks (1967–77),
Cleveland Cavaliers (1977–79)

Games: 825 **RPG:** 5.9
Points: 15,581 **Assists:** 5,040
PPG: 18.9 **APG:** 6.1
Rebounds:
4,830
Awards: Seven All-Star Games, First-Team All-NBA (1970, 1972, 1974, 1975)

A stylish figure on and off the court, Walt Frazier was a perfect fit for New York City and the Knicks. As a point guard, he made the Knicks run, but he also contributed to scoring with well-timed drives to the basket and a savage pull-up jumper. Frazier was named to the NBA All-Defensive first team for seven consecutive years. He led the Knicks to NBA titles in 1970 and 1973.

Kevin Garnett

KEVIN GARNETT F

Minnesota Timberwolves (1995–2007, 2015–16), Boston Celtics (2007–13), Brooklyn Nets (2013–15)

Kevin Garnett was a high school senior when the Timberwolves selected him with the fifth pick of the 1995 NBA Draft. He developed into one of the game's most well-rounded players. He averaged at least 20 points, ten assists, and five rebounds for six straight seasons. He also was named to the NBA All-Defensive first team nine times. Garnett helped put the Celtics over the top as they won the 2008 NBA title.

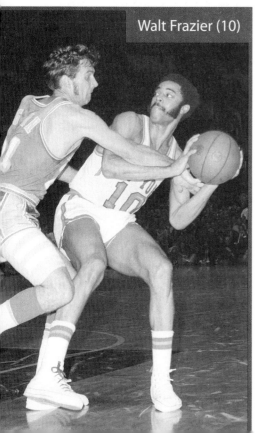
Walt Frazier (10)

Games: 1,462	**Assists:** 5,445
Points: 26,071	**APG:** 3.7
PPG: 17.8	**Blocked shots:**
Rebounds:	2,037
14,662	**Steals:** 1,859
RPG: 10	

Awards: NBA MVP (2004), NBA Defensive Player of the Year (2008), 15 All-Star Games, First-Team All-NBA (2000, 2003, 2004, 2008)

George Gervin (44)

GEORGE GERVIN G-F

Virginia Squires [ABA] (1972–74), San Antonio Spurs [ABA] (1974–76), San Antonio Spurs (1976–85), Chicago Bulls (1985–86)

A graceful and creative scorer, George Gervin's patented finger roll helped him win four NBA scoring titles. He posted a career-high 33.1 points per game in 1979–80. Gervin also was spot-on at the line, hitting more than 84 percent of his career free throws.

Games: 1,060
Points: 26,595
PPG: 25.1
Rebounds: 5,602
RPG: 5.3
Assists: 2,798
APG: 2.6
Blocked shots: 1,047
Steals: 1,283
Awards: Twelve All-Star Games, First-Team All-NBA (1978–82)

JAMES HARDEN G

Oklahoma City Thunder (2009–12), Houston Rockets (2012–21), Brooklyn Nets (2021–)

Known for his bushy beard and smooth left-handed jumper, James Harden made himself into one of the most feared offensive

Games: 877
Points: 22,045
PPG: 25.1
Rebounds: 4,794
RPG: 5.5
Assists: 5,730
APG: 6.5
Blocked shots: 476
Steals: 1,367
Awards: NBA MVP (2018), NBA Sixth Man of the Year (2012), nine All-Star Games, First-Team All-NBA (2014, 2015, 2017–20)

weapons in the NBA. He came off the bench for three seasons in Oklahoma City and earned an NBA Sixth Man of the Year Award before leaving for Houston. With the Rockets, Harden proved that he could do it all on offense. He led the NBA in assists in 2016–17. Then he won the NBA scoring title the next three seasons, averaging 33.7 points per game.

James Harden

JOHN HAVLICEK F

Boston Celtics (1962–78)

John Havlicek might not have been the team leader in any statistical category, but he held the Celtics together on the court. Havlicek was a five-time member of the NBA All-Defensive first team. He also was one of the first players to embrace the sixth man role, coming off the bench to provide whatever the Celtics needed that night. Later in his career, Havlicek took on more of a scoring role. He led Boston to the NBA title in 1974, averaging 27 points per game in the playoffs.

John Havlicek

Games: 1,270   **RPG:** 6.3
Points: 26,395   **Assists:** 6,114
PPG: 20.8   **APG:** 4.8
Rebounds: 8,007
Awards: NBA Finals MVP (1974), 13 All-Star Games, First-Team All-NBA (1971–74)

ELVIN HAYES F-C

San Diego Rockets (1968–71), Houston Rockets (1971–72, 1981–84), Baltimore Bullets (1972–73), Capital Bullets (1973–74), Washington Bullets (1974–81)

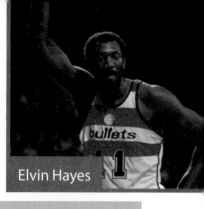

Elvin Hayes

Elvin Hayes was the NBA scoring champion as a rookie with the San Diego Rockets. He was one of the most durable players of his era, never playing in fewer than 80 games in any of his 16 NBA seasons. Using his unstoppable turnaround jumper, Hayes was practically a guaranteed

Games:	Rebounds:
1,303	16,279
Points:	**RPG:** 12.5
27,313	**Assists:** 2,398
PPG: 21	**APG:** 1.8

Awards: Twelve All-Star Games, First-Team All-NBA (1975, 1977, 1979)

double-double. He averaged two blocked shots per game as well. Hayes helped lead the Bullets to the NBA Finals three times, finally winning a title in 1978.

ALLEN IVERSON G

Philadelphia 76ers (1996–2006, 2009–10), Denver Nuggets (2006–08), Detroit Pistons (2008–09), Memphis Grizzlies (2009)

Games: 914	RPG: 3.7
Points: 24,368	**Assists:** 5,624
PPG: 26.7	**APG:** 6.2
Rebounds: 3,394	**Steals:** 1,983

Awards: NBA Rookie of the Year (1997), NBA MVP (2001), 11 All-Star Games, First-Team All-NBA (1999, 2001, 2005)

Allen Iverson put every bit of his 6-foot, 165-pound body on the line whenever he stepped onto the court. A dynamic ball handler with a deadly crossover dribble, Iverson's fearless drives to the basket and graceful finishes became a trademark. He's one of five players with at least four NBA scoring titles. Iverson led the league in steals three times as well.

LeBRON JAMES G-F

Cleveland Cavaliers (2003–10, 2014–18), Miami Heat (2010–14), Los Angeles Lakers (2018–)

LeBron James was a huge scorer who also racked up more than seven rebounds and assists per night. James almost single-handedly made the Cavs NBA champions. He also reached the NBA Finals four times and won two titles with the Heat. In addition, he brought the Lakers their first championship in a decade when they beat Miami in the 2020 Finals.

Games: 1,310
Points: 35,367
PPG: 27
Rebounds: 9,751
RPG: 7.4
Assists: 9,696
APG: 7.4
Blocked shots: 982
Steals: 2,063
Awards: NBA Rookie of the Year (2004), NBA MVP (2009, 2010, 2012, 2013), NBA Finals MVP (2012, 2013, 2016, 2020), 17 All-Star Games, First-Team All-NBA (2006, 2008–18, 2020)

Allen Iverson

LeBron James

163

EARVIN "MAGIC" JOHNSON G

*Los Angeles Lakers
(1979–91, 1996)*

Blessed with a catchy nickname and a gleaming smile, Earvin "Magic" Johnson was a natural fit for the spotlight. More than any player, he was responsible for the success of the "Showtime" Lakers, who won five NBA titles in the 1980s. Whether setting up a teammate for a dunk on the fast break or running the offense with precision, few point guards have ever had a better feel for the game than Johnson. He retired as the NBA's all-time leader in assists per game.

Games: 906 **RPG**: 7.2
Points: 17,707 **Assists**: 10,141
PPG: 19.5 **APG**: 11.2
Rebounds: 6,559 **Steals**: 1,724
Awards: NBA MVP (1987, 1989, 1990), NBA Finals MVP (1980, 1982, 1987), 12 All-Star Games, First-Team All-NBA (1983–91)

Earvin "Magic" Johnson

MICHAEL JORDAN G

*Chicago Bulls (1984–93, 1995–98),
Washington Wizards (2001–03)*

Michael Jordan wanted to win, and he was willing to put in whatever work needed to put his team over the top. It helped that he also had elite leaping ability, lightning-quick hands, and one of the sharpest minds the game has ever seen. Jordan carried the Bulls to the playoffs six times before they won their first title. Then they won six championships in his last six full seasons with the team. Whether soaring through the air for a dunk with his tongue hanging out or coolly sinking a game-winning jumper, perhaps no NBA player has ever been more iconic than Jordan.

Games: 1,072
Points: 32,292
PPG: 30.1
Rebounds: 6,672
RPG: 6.2

Assists: 5,633
APG: 5.3
Blocked shots: 893
Steals: 2,514

Awards: NBA Rookie of the Year (1985), NBA MVP (1988, 1989, 1991, 1992, 1996, 1998), NBA Finals MVP (1991–93, 1996–98), NBA Defensive Player of the Year (1988), 14 All-Star Games, First-Team All-NBA (1987–93, 1996–98)

Michael Jordan

JASON KIDD G

Dallas Mavericks (1994–96, 2008–12), Phoenix Suns (1996–2001), New Jersey Nets (2001–08), New York Knicks (2012–13)

Jason Kidd wasn't a huge scorer, but thanks to his passing skills, many of his teammates were. Kidd was a point guard who didn't need to score to be effective, but he did have a knack for timely scoring. He posted 14.7 and 18.7 points in back-to-back seasons as he led the Nets to the NBA Finals. He led the NBA in assists five times and retired with the second-most assists and steals in NBA history.

Jason Kidd

Games: 1,391
Points: 17,529
PPG: 12.6
Rebounds: 8,725
RPG: 6.3
Assists: 12,091
APG: 8.7
Steals: 2,684
Awards: NBA Rookie of the Year (1995), ten All-Star Games, First-Team All-NBA (1999–2002, 2004)

Kawhi Leonard

KAWHI LEONARD F

San Antonio Spurs (2011–18), Toronto Raptors (2018–19), Los Angeles Clippers (2019–)

Games: 576 **RPG:** 6.4
Points: 11,085 **Assists:** 1,672
PPG: 19.2 **APG:** 2.9
Rebounds: 3,689 **Steals:** 1,013
Awards: NBA Finals MVP (2014, 2019), NBA Defensive Player of the Year (2015, 2016), five All-Star Games, First-Team All-NBA (2016, 2017)

Kawhi Leonard was a mid-first-round pick in the 2011 draft. He averaged less than 20 points per game in each of his first four seasons. However, his defense set him apart. He was a three-time NBA All-Defensive first team member. He also earned the MVP Award in the 2014 Finals. The Raptors traded for Leonard in 2018. He led them to the NBA title, averaging 26.6 points and 7.3 rebounds per game. He then took his talents to Los Angeles, where he averaged 26 points per game in his first two seasons with the Clippers.

KARL MALONE F

Utah Jazz (1985–2003), Los Angeles Lakers (2003–04)

Karl Malone was a bruising presence who used his 6-foot-9, 250-pound frame to bully the opposition. Malone missed only ten games in 18 seasons with the Jazz. He and point guard John Stockton perfected the pick-and-roll, a move that seems unstoppable if executed to perfection. Malone retired with more points than anyone other than Kareem Abdul-Jabbar and is the NBA career leader in free throws.

Karl Malone

Games: 1,476 **RPG:** 10.1
Points: 36,928 **Assists:** 5,248
PPG: 25.0 **APG:** 3.6
Rebounds: 14,968 **Blocked shots:** 1,145
Steals: 2,085
Awards: NBA MVP (1997, 1999), 14 All-Star Games, First-Team All-NBA (1989–99)

Moses Malone, *right*

MOSES MALONE c

Utah Stars [ABA] (1974–75), Spirits of St. Louis [ABA] (1975–76), Buffalo Braves (1976), Houston Rockets (1976–82), Philadelphia 76ers (1982–86, 1993–94), Washington Bullets (1986–88), Atlanta Hawks (1988–91), Milwaukee Bucks (1991–93), San Antonio Spurs (1994)

Moses Malone was the first modern player to go straight from high school to the professional ranks. It didn't take him long to get used to the pro game. He averaged 18.8 points and 14.6 rebounds per game as a rookie in the ABA. Malone dominated the low post like few players of his era. He led the NBA in rebounding six times and was the key figure in leading the 76ers to the NBA title in his first season in Philadelphia.

Games: 1,455   **RPG:** 12.3
Points: 29,580   **Assists:** 1,936
PPG: 20.3   **Blocked shots:** 1,889
Rebounds: 17,834   **Steals:** 1,199
Awards: NBA MVP (1979, 1982, 1983),
NBA Finals MVP (1983), 13 All-Star Games,
First-Team All-NBA (1979, 1982, 1983, 1985)

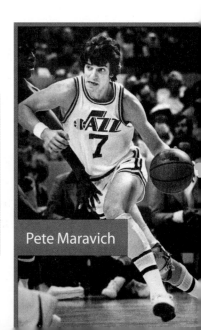

Pete Maravich

168

PETE MARAVICH G

*Atlanta Hawks (1970–74),
New Orleans Jazz (1974–79),
Utah Jazz (1979), Boston
Celtics (1980)*

Games: 658	**RPG:** 4.2
Points: 15,948	**Assists:** 3,563
PPG: 24.2	**APG:** 5.4
Rebounds: 2,747	
Awards: Five All-Star Games, First-Team All-NBA (1976, 1977)	

Pete Maravich was a sensation coming out of Louisiana State University. The skinny kid with the floppy hair averaged a record 44.2 points per game in college. He brought that offensive mindset to the NBA, wowing fans with his no-look passes and pull-up jumpers from nearly anywhere on the court. Maravich led the NBA in scoring with 31.1 points per game in 1976–77. But his artistry on the court was more important than any statistic could ever capture.

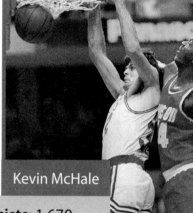

Kevin McHale

KEVIN McHALE F

Boston Celtics (1980–93)

Games: 971	**Assists:** 1,670
Points: 17,335	**APG:** 1.7
PPG: 17.9	**Blocked shots:** 1,690
Rebounds: 7,122	
RPG: 7.3	
Awards: NBA Sixth Man of the Year (1984, 1985), seven All-Star Games, First-Team All-NBA (1987)	

Kevin McHale teamed with Larry Bird and Robert Parish to form one of the toughest front lines in NBA history. McHale's long arms and precise footwork made him difficult to defend in the low block. And his fadeaway jumper was nearly unstoppable. McHale came off the bench to help the Celtics win NBA titles in 1981 and 1984. By 1986, he'd broken into the starting lineup. His 21.7 points and 8.3 rebounds per game helped the Celtics win yet another title.

GEORGE MIKAN C

Minneapolis Lakers
(1948–54, 1956)

George Mikan

George Mikan was professional basketball's first superstar. He won championships with the Lakers in the NBL, BAA, and NBA. At 6-foot-10, he towered over most of his opponents, and he was responsible for many rule changes, including a wider lane and the ban on goaltending.

Games: 439
Points: 10,156
PPG: 23.1
Rebounds: 4,167
RPG: 13.4
Assists: 1,245
APG: 2.8
Awards: Four All-Star Games, First-Team All-BAA (1949), First-Team All-NBA (1950–54)

REGGIE MILLER G

Indiana Pacers
(1987–2005)

Games: 1,389
Points: 25,279
PPG: 18.2
Three-pointers: 2,560
Three-pointers per game: 1.8
Rebounds: 4,182
RPG: 3.0
Assists: 4,141
APG: 3.0
Steals: 2,409
Awards: Five All-Star Games

Reggie Miller was one of the NBA's ultimate sharpshooters. He seemed to thrive in the clutch, coming up big when the Indiana Pacers needed him the most. And the bigger the spotlight, the better he seemed to play. Miller famously scored eight points in nine seconds to help Indiana defeat the Knicks in Game 1 of the 1995 Eastern Conference semifinals. He retired as the NBA's all-time leader in three-pointers. Miller also led the league in free-throw percentage five times.

Reggie Miller

Steve Nash

STEVE NASH G

Phoenix Suns (1996–98, 2004–12), Dallas Mavericks (1998–2004), Los Angeles Lakers (2012–14)

Games: 1,217	**RPG:** 3.0
Points: 17,387	**Assists:** 10,335
PPG: 14.3	**APG:** 8.5
Rebounds: 3,642	**Steals:** 899
Awards: NBA MVP (2005, 2006), eight All-Star Games, First-Team All-NBA (2005–07)	

One of two Canadian-born players enshrined in the Basketball Hall of Fame, Steve Nash was something of a late bloomer. Nash led the NBA in assists for the first time at age 30. Then he did it four more times. He wasn't just an elite passer, however. Nash is the only four-time member of the 50–40–90 club, meaning he made at least 50 percent of his shots from the floor, 40 percent of his three-pointers, and 90 percent of his free throws for an entire season.

DIRK NOWITZKI F

Dallas Mavericks (1998–2019)

Dirk Nowitzki was the NBA's first superstar from Germany. He averaged at least 20 points per game in 13 of his 20 NBA seasons. The 7-footer had an excellent shooting touch. He averaged 38 percent on three-pointers and 88 percent on free throws throughout his career. He led the Mavericks in scoring for 14 straight seasons. He also played in two NBA Finals, winning the series MVP Award in 2011 when he averaged 26 points and 9.7 rebounds as the Mavs defeated Miami in six games.

Games: 1,522
Points: 31,560
PPG: 20.7
Rebounds: 11,489
RPG: 7.5
Assists: 3,651
APG: 2.4
Blocked shots: 1,281
Steals: 1,210
Awards: NBA MVP (2007), NBA Finals MVP (2011), 14 All-Star Games, First-Team All-NBA (2005–07, 2009)

Dirk Nowitzki

HAKEEM OLAJUWON c

Houston Rockets (1984–2001),
Toronto Raptors (2001–02)

Hakeem Olajuwon became one of the greatest centers in the history of basketball. Through 2021, "Hakeem the Dream" was the all-time leader in blocked shots. Plus, he was the only player with at least 3,000 blocked shots and 2,000 steals in his career. Olajuwon led the Rockets to back-to-back NBA titles. This was largely due to his dominant defense and slick offensive moves near the basket.

Games: 1,238
Points: 26,946
PPG: 21.8
Rebounds: 13,748
RPG: 11.1

Assists: 3,058
APG: 2.5
Blocked shots: 3,830
Steals: 2,162

Awards: NBA MVP (1994), NBA Finals MVP (1994, 1995), NBA Defensive Player of the Year (1993, 1994), 12 All-Star Games, First-Team All-NBA (1987–89, 1993, 1994, 1997)

Hakeem Olajuwon

SHAQUILLE O'NEAL c

Orlando Magic (1992–96), Los Angeles Lakers (1996–2004), Miami Heat (2004–08), Phoenix Suns (2008–09), Cleveland Cavaliers (2009–10), Boston Celtics (2010–11)

Shaquille O'Neal was the center of attention every time he stepped onto the court. He filled up the stat sheet, averaging 26.7 points and 12 rebounds per game in his first 13 NBA seasons. Nearly unstoppable when he got the ball close to the hoop, O'Neal led the league in field-goal percentage ten times. He teamed up with Kobe Bryant to lead the Lakers to three straight NBA titles, winning the Finals MVP Award each year. O'Neal also picked up another ring with the Heat in 2006.

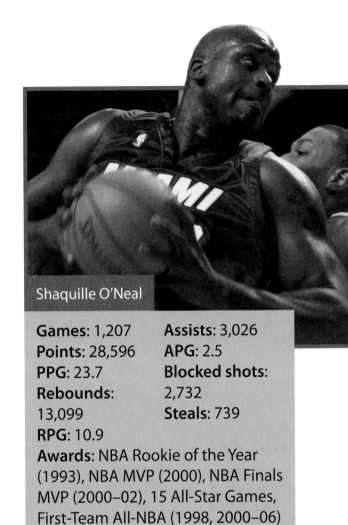

Shaquille O'Neal

Games: 1,207
Points: 28,596
PPG: 23.7
Rebounds: 13,099
RPG: 10.9
Assists: 3,026
APG: 2.5
Blocked shots: 2,732
Steals: 739
Awards: NBA Rookie of the Year (1993), NBA MVP (2000), NBA Finals MVP (2000–02), 15 All-Star Games, First-Team All-NBA (1998, 2000–06)

Chris Paul

CHRIS PAUL G

New Orleans/Oklahoma City Hornets (2005–07), New Orleans Hornets (2007–11), Los Angeles Clippers (2011–17), Houston Rockets (2017–19), Oklahoma City Thunder (2019–20), Phoenix Suns (2020–)

Chris Paul turned himself into a two-way threat, leading the league in assists four times and in steals six times. He also became an elite free-throw shooter and a seven-time NBA All-Defensive first team member. Paul helped lead the Phoenix Suns to the Western Conference finals and then to the NBA Finals in 2021.

Games: 1,090 **RPG:** 4.5
Points: 19,978 **Assists:** 10,275
PPG: 18.3 **APG:** 9.4
Rebounds: 4,923 **Steals:** 2,332
Awards: NBA Rookie of the Year (2006), 11 All-Star Games, First-Team All-NBA (2008, 2012–14)

BOB PETTIT F

Milwaukee Hawks (1954–55), St. Louis Hawks (1955–65)

Bob Pettit

An All-Star in each of his 11 NBA seasons, Bob Pettit helped revolutionize the role of the power forward. He used his 6-foot-9 frame to average 16.2 rebounds per game over his career. But he also was an elite offensive player who won two NBA scoring titles. Pettit was the face of the Hawks his entire career. He reached his peak in 1958 when he led the club to the NBA title, averaging 29.3 points and 17 rebounds as the Hawks knocked off the Celtics in the Finals.

Games: 792 **Rebounds:** 12,849 **APG:** 3
Points: 20,880 **RPG:** 16.2
PPG: 26.4 **Assists:** 2,369
Awards: NBA Rookie of the Year (1955), NBA MVP (1956, 1959), 11 All-Star Games, First-Team All-NBA (1955–64)

Scottie Pippen

SCOTTIE PIPPEN F

Chicago Bulls (1987–98, 2003–04), Houston Rockets (1999), Portland Trail Blazers (1999–2003)

Michael Jordan may have been the face of the Chicago Bulls, but he never won a championship without Scottie Pippen at his side. Pippen provided secondary scoring and elite defense to the Bulls teams that won six NBA titles in eight seasons. He was an eight-time All-Defensive first team pick who thrived on the fast break. Pippen won two Olympic gold medals, including one with the Dream Team at the 1992 Olympics. He was the youngest NBA veteran to be selected for that dynamic US team.

Games: 1,178	**Rebounds:** 7,494	**APG:** 5.2
Points: 18,940	**RPG:** 6.4	**Blocked shots:** 947
PPG: 16.1	**Assists:** 6,135	**Steals:** 2,307
Awards: Seven All-Star Games, First-Team All-NBA (1994–96)		

OSCAR ROBERTSON G

Cincinnati Royals (1960–70), Milwaukee Bucks (1970–74)

Oscar Robertson helped revolutionize the role of the point guard. Before he joined the NBA, point guards mostly focused on running the offense and setting up their teammates for baskets. Robertson showed that point guards could score and grab rebounds as well. In 1961–62, he was the first player to average a triple-double for an entire season. He also led the league in scoring once and in assists seven times.

Games: 1,040	**Rebounds:** 7,804
Points: 26,710	**RPG:** 7.5
PPG: 25.7	**Assists:** 9,887
	APG: 9.5
Awards: NBA Rookie of the Year (1961), NBA MVP (1964), 12 All-Star Games, First-Team All-NBA (1961–69)	

DAVID ROBINSON C

*San Antonio Spurs
(1989–2003)*

David Robinson was the unquestioned leader of the Spurs. He helped the team win NBA titles in 1999 and 2003. Robinson won a scoring title and a rebounding title, and he also led the NBA in blocked shots in 1992. He was a member of the Dream Team that won gold at the 1992 Olympics. He won gold again four years later.

David Robinson

Oscar Robertson (14)

Games: 987
Points: 20,790
PPG: 21.1
Rebounds: 10,497
RPG: 10.6
Assists: 2,441
APG: 2.5
Blocked shots: 2,954
Steals: 1,388

Awards: NBA Rookie of the Year (1990), NBA MVP (1995), NBA Defensive Player of the Year (1992), ten All-Star Games, First-Team All-NBA (1991–92, 1995–96)

Bill Russell

BILL RUSSELL C

Boston Celtics (1956–69)

Few players were more used to winning than Bill Russell during his NBA career. His Celtics teams won 11 NBA titles during his 13 seasons. The last two titles came when he was serving as a player-coach. Russell redefined the role of the defensive center. He led the NBA in rebounding five times and earned multiple NBA MVP Awards.

Games: 963 **RPG:** 22.5
Points: 14,522 **Assists:** 4,100
PPG: 15.1 **APG:** 4.3
Rebounds: 21,620
Awards: NBA MVP (1958, 1961–63, 1965), 12 All-Star Games, First-Team All-NBA (1959, 1963, 1965)

JOHN STOCKTON G

Utah Jazz (1984–2003)

John Stockton was the NBA's model point guard for two decades. Teaming with power forward Karl Malone, Stockton helped the Utah Jazz reach the NBA Finals twice. He led the NBA in assists nine straight seasons and is the NBA's all-time leader in career assists and steals. Stockton led the Jazz to the playoffs in each of his 19 seasons. He was also a key part of the 1992 US Dream Team that won the gold medal at the Olympics.

Games: 1,504 **RPG:** 2.7
Points: 19,711 **Assists:** 15,806
PPG: 13.1
Rebounds: 4,051 **APG:** 10.5
Steals: 3,265
Awards: Ten All-Star Games, First-Team All-NBA (1994, 1995)

John Stockton

ISIAH THOMAS G

Detroit Pistons (1981–94)

A creative scorer and elite passer, Isiah Thomas was the engine driving the Detroit Pistons for 13 seasons. Thomas averaged 20 points and ten assists in four straight seasons as the Pistons built a championship team. Then he was the team's floor general as Detroit won back-to-back NBA titles in 1989 and 1990.

Games: 979   **RPG:** 3.6
Points: 18,822   **Assists:** 9,061
PPG: 19.2   **APG:** 9.3
Rebounds: 3,478   **Steals:** 1,861
Awards: NBA Finals MVP (1990), 12 All-Star Games, First-Team All-NBA (1984–86)

Isiah Thomas

BILL WALTON c

Portland Trail Blazers (1974–78), San Diego Clippers (1980–84), Los Angeles Clippers (1984–85), Boston Celtics (1985–87)

Bill Walton fought through many injuries to forge a Hall of Fame career. No one can say what kind of numbers he might have put up if his feet and knees had stayed healthy. But despite his physical struggles, Walton made his mark on the basketball world. He was a two-time NCAA champion at the University of California, Los Angeles. Walton was also a two-time NBA champion. He was the focal point of Portland's 1977 title team. He later proved to be a valuable asset as he helped the Celtics win another ring in 1986.

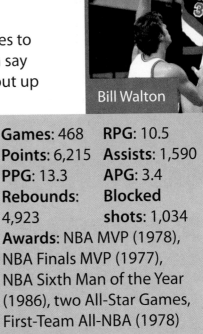

Bill Walton

Games: 468   **RPG:** 10.5
Points: 6,215   **Assists:** 1,590
PPG: 13.3   **APG:** 3.4
Rebounds: 4,923   **Blocked shots:** 1,034
Awards: NBA MVP (1978), NBA Finals MVP (1977), NBA Sixth Man of the Year (1986), two All-Star Games, First-Team All-NBA (1978)

Jerry West (44)

JERRY WEST G

Los Angeles Lakers (1960–74)

Jerry West was one of the game's all-time great shooters while also earning four berths on the NBA's All-Defensive first team. When West retired, he was among the top five in career points, scoring average, free throws, and assists. He went on to a successful post-retirement career in the front office of the Lakers and Memphis Grizzlies. He won the NBA Executive of the Year award with each team.

Games: 932 **RPG:** 5.8
Points: 25,192 **Assists:** 6,238
PPG: 27 **APG:** 6.7
Rebounds: 5,366
Awards: NBA Finals MVP (1969), 14 All-Star Games, First-Team All-NBA (1962–67, 1970–73)

RUSSELL WESTBROOK G

Oklahoma City Thunder (2008–19), Houston Rockets (2019–20), Washington Wizards (2020– 21), Los Angeles Lakers (2021–)

Russell Westbrook has left his mark on the game as one of the top multitalented players of all time. Before Westbrook came into the league, only Oscar Robertson had averaged a triple-double over the course of an entire season—and he did it only once. In 2020–21, Westbrook accomplished that feat for the fourth time. Along the way, he led the NBA in scoring twice and in assists three times. His career mark of 184 triple-doubles (and counting) is an NBA record.

Games: 943 **RPG:** 7.4
Points: 21,857 **Assists:** 8,061
PPG: 23.2 **APG:** 8.5
Rebounds: 6,961 **Steals:** 1,624
Awards: NBA MVP (2017), nine All-Star Games, First-Team All-NBA (2016, 2017)

Russell Westbrook

Dominique Wilkins (21)

DOMINIQUE WILKINS F

Atlanta Hawks (1982–94), Los Angeles Clippers (1994), Boston Celtics (1994–95), San Antonio Spurs (1996–97), Orlando Magic (1999)

Dominique Wilkins was called the "Human Highlight Film" because of his electrifying dunks. He was an elite scorer who could drain long jumpers as easily as he could blow past a defender for an easy two points. Wilkins waged epic battles with Michael Jordan of the Bulls and Boston's Larry Bird. He reminded NBA fans that artistry was as much a part of the game as athleticism.

Games: 1,074
Points: 26,668
PPG: 24.8
Rebounds: 7,169
RPG: 6.7

Assists: 2,677
APG: 2.5
Blocked shots: 642
Steals: 1,378

Awards: Nine All-Star Games, First-Team All-NBA (1986)

182

James Worthy

JAMES WORTHY F

Los Angeles Lakers (1982–94)

James Worthy wasn't a flashy player, but he thrived as a key part of the Lakers' "Showtime" era. He was equally skilled at finishing a fast break with a windmill dunk or scoring from the low block in the half-court offense. Worthy developed a reputation as a clutch player for the Lakers as he helped lead them to three NBA titles during his 12 seasons in Los Angeles.

Games: 926
Points: 16,320
PPG: 17.6
Rebounds: 4,708
RPG: 5.1
Assists: 2,791
APG: 3
Blocked shots: 624
Steals: 1,041
Awards: NBA Finals MVP (1988), seven All-Star Games

HONORABLE MENTIONS

Carmelo Anthony (F): Denver Nuggets (2003–11), New York Knicks (2011–17), Oklahoma City Thunder (2017–18), Houston Rockets (2018), Portland Trail Blazers (2019–21), Los Angeles Lakers (2021–)

Nate Archibald (G): Cincinnati Royals (1970–72), Kansas City-Omaha Kings (1972–75), Kansas City Kings (1975–76), New York Nets (1976–77), Boston Celtics (1978–83), Milwaukee Bucks (1983–84)

Paul Arizin (F): Philadelphia Warriors (1950–62)

Chauncey Billups (G): Boston Celtics (1997–98), Toronto Raptors (1998), Denver Nuggets (1998–2000, 2008–11), Minnesota Timberwolves (2000–02), Detroit Pistons (2002–08, 2013–14), New York Knicks (2011), Los Angeles Clippers (2011–13)

Vince Carter (F-G): Toronto Raptors (1999–04), New Jersey Nets (2004–09), Orlando Magic (2009–10), Phoenix Suns (2010–11), Dallas Mavericks (2011–14), Memphis Grizzlies (2014–17), Sacramento Kings (2017–18), Atlanta Hawks (2018–20)

Dave Cowens (C): Boston Celtics (1970–80), Milwaukee Bucks (1982–83)

Adrian Dantley (F): Buffalo Braves (1976–77), Indiana Pacers (1977), Los Angeles Lakers (1977–79), Utah Jazz (1979–86), Detroit Pistons (1986–89), Dallas Mavericks (1989–90), Milwaukee Bucks (1991)

Anthony Davis (F-C): New Orleans Hornets (2012–13), New Orleans Pelicans (2013–19), Los Angeles Lakers (2019–)

Dave DeBusschere (F): Detroit Pistons (1962–68), New York Knicks (1968–74)

Clyde Drexler (G): Portland Trail Blazers (1983–95), Houston Rockets (1995–98)

Joe Dumars (G): Detroit Pistons (1985–99)

Alex English (F): Milwaukee Bucks (1976–78), Indiana Pacers (1978–80), Denver Nuggets (1980–90), Dallas Mavericks (1990–91)

Pau Gasol (F-C): Memphis Grizzlies (2001–08), Los Angeles Lakers (2008–14), Chicago Bulls (2014–16), San Antonio Spurs (2016–19), Milwaukee Bucks (2019)

Paul George (F-G): Indiana Pacers (2010–17), Oklahoma City Thunder (2017–19), Los Angeles Clippers (2019–)

Artis Gilmore (C): Kentucky Colonels [ABA] (1971–76), Chicago Bulls (1976–82, 1987), San Antonio Spurs (1982–87), Boston Celtics (1988)

Manu Ginóbili (G): San Antonio Spurs (2002–18)

Gail Goodrich (G): Los Angeles Lakers (1965–68, 1970–76), Phoenix Suns (1968–70), New Orleans Jazz (1976–79)

Hal Greer (G): Syracuse Nationals (1958–63), Philadelphia 76ers (1963–73)

Grant Hill (F): Detroit Pistons (1994–2000), Orlando Magic (2000–07), Phoenix Suns (2007–12), Los Angeles Clippers (2012–13)

Dwight Howard (C): Orlando Magic (2004–12), Los Angeles Lakers (2012–13, 2019–20), Houston Rockets (2013–16), Atlanta Hawks (2016–17), Charlotte Hornets (2017–18), Washington Wizards (2018–19), Philadelphia 76ers (2020–21), Los Angeles Lakers (2021–)

Kyrie Irving (G): Cleveland Cavaliers (2011–17), Boston Celtics (2017–19), Brooklyn Nets (2019–)

Dennis Johnson (G): Seattle SuperSonics (1976–80), Phoenix Suns (1980–83), Boston Celtics (1983–90)

Sam Jones (G-F): Boston Celtics (1957–69)

Bernard King (F): New Jersey Nets (1977–79, 1993), Utah Jazz (1979), Golden State Warriors (1980–82), New York Knicks (1982–87), Washington Bullets (1987–91)

Bob Lanier (C): Detroit Pistons (1970–80), Milwaukee Bucks (1980–84)

Damian Lillard (G): Portland Trail Blazers (2012–)

Jerry Lucas (F): Cincinnati Royals (1963–69), San Francisco Warriors (1969–71), New York Knicks (1971–74)

Bob McAdoo (F-C): Buffalo Braves (1972–76), New York Knicks (1976–79), Boston Celtics (1979), Detroit Pistons (1979–81), New Jersey Nets (1981), Los Angeles Lakers (1981–85), Philadelphia 76ers (1986)

Tracy McGrady (G-F): Toronto Raptors (1997–2000), Orlando Magic (2000–04), Houston Rockets (2004–10), New York Knicks (2010), Detroit Pistons (2010–11), Atlanta Hawks (2011–12)

Vern Mikkelsen (F): Minneapolis Lakers (1949–59)

Earl Monroe (G): Baltimore Bullets (1967–71), New York Knicks (1971–80)

Alonzo Mourning (C): Charlotte Hornets (1992–95), Miami Heat (1995–2002, 2005–08), New Jersey Nets (2003–04)

Chris Mullin (F): Golden State Warriors (1985–97, 2000–01), Indiana Pacers (1997–2000)

Dikembe Mutombo (C): Denver Nuggets (1991–96), Atlanta Hawks (1996–2001), Philadelphia 76ers (2001–02), New Jersey Nets (2002–03), New York Knicks (2003–04), Houston Rockets (2004–09)

Robert Parish (C): Golden State Warriors (1976–80), Boston Celtics (1980–94), Charlotte Hornets (1994–96), Chicago Bulls (1996–97)

Tony Parker (G): San Antonio Spurs (2001–18), Charlotte Hornets (2018–19)

Gary Payton (G): Seattle SuperSonics (1990–2003), Milwaukee Bucks (2003), Los Angeles Lakers (2003–04), Boston Celtics (2004–05), Miami Heat (2005–07)

Paul Pierce (F): Boston Celtics (1999–2013), Brooklyn Nets (2013–14), Washington Wizards (2014–15), Los Angeles Clippers (2015–17)

Willis Reed (C-F): New York Knicks (1964–74)

Mitch Richmond (G): Golden State Warriors (1988–91), Sacramento Kings (1991–98), Washington Wizards (1999–2001), Los Angeles Lakers (2001–02)

Dennis Rodman (F): Detroit Pistons (1986–93), San Antonio Spurs (1993–95), Chicago Bulls (1995–98), Los Angeles Lakers (1999), Dallas Mavericks (2000)

Dolph Schayes (F): Syracuse Nationals (1949–63), Philadelphia 76ers (1963–64)

Bill Sharman (G): Washington Capitols (1950–51), Boston Celtics (1951–61)

David Thompson (G): Denver Nuggets [ABA] (1975–76), Denver Nuggets (1976–82), Seattle SuperSonics (1982–84)

Klay Thompson (G): Golden State Warriors (2011–)

Nate Thurmond (C): San Francisco Warriors (1963–71), Golden State Warriors (1971–74), Chicago Bulls (1974–75), Cleveland Cavaliers (1975–77)

Wes Unseld (C): Baltimore Bullets (1968–73), Capital Bullets (1973–74), Washington Bullets (1974–81)

Dwyane Wade (G): Miami Heat (2003–16, 2018–19), Chicago Bulls (2016–17), Cleveland Cavaliers (2017–18)

Chris Webber (F): Golden State Warriors (1993–94, 2008), Washington Bullets (1994–97), Washington Wizards (1997–98), Sacramento Kings (1999–2005), Philadelphia 76ers (2005–07), Detroit Pistons (2007)

Lenny Wilkens (G): St. Louis Hawks (1960–68), Seattle SuperSonics (1968–72), Cleveland Cavaliers (1972–74), Portland Trail Blazers, (1974–75)

Madison Square Garden

GAMES PLAYED

1. Robert Parish _____ 1,611
2. Kareem Abdul-Jabbar _____ 1,560
3. Vince Carter _____ 1,541
4. Dirk Nowitzki _____ 1,522
5. John Stockton _____ 1,504

POINTS

1. Kareem Abdul-Jabbar _____ 38,387
2. Karl Malone _____ 36,928
3. LeBron James* _____ 35,367
4. Kobe Bryant _____ 33,643
5. Michael Jordan _____ 32,292

POINTS PER GAME

1. Michael Jordan _____ 30.12
2. Wilt Chamberlain _____ 30.07
3. Elgin Baylor _____ 27.36
4. Jerry West _____ 27.03
5. Kevin Durant* _____ 27.02

FIELD GOALS

1. Kareem Abdul-Jabbar _____ 15,837
2. Karl Malone _____ 13,528
3. LeBron James* _____ 12,903
4. Wilt Chamberlain _____ 12,681
5. Michael Jordan _____ 12,192

FIELD-GOAL PERCENTAGE

1. DeAndre Jordan* _____ .674
2. Rudy Gobert* _____ .645
3. Clint Capela* _____ .626
4. Montrezl Harrell* _____ .616
5. Tyson Chandler _____ .597

THREE-POINTERS

1. Ray Allen _____ 2,973
2. Stephen Curry* _____ 2,832
3. Reggie Miller _____ 2,560
4. Kyle Korver _____ 2,450
5. James Harden* _____ 2,445

THREE-POINT PERCENTAGE

1. Steve Kerr _____ .454
2. Seth Curry* _____ .444
3. Hubert Davis _____ .441
4. Joe Harris* _____ .438
5. Dražen Petrović _____ .437

FREE THROWS

1. Karl Malone _____ 9,787
2. Moses Malone _____ 9,018
3. Kobe Bryant _____ 8,378
4. Oscar Robertson _____ 7,694
5. LeBron James* _____ 7,582

FREE-THROW PERCENTAGE

1. Stephen Curry* _____ .9069
2. Steve Nash _____ .9043
3. Mark Price _____ .9039
4. Peja Stojaković _____ .8948
5. Chauncey Billups _____ .8940

REBOUNDS
1. Wilt Chamberlain _____ 23,924
2. Bill Russell _____ 21,620
3. Moses Malone _____ 17,834
4. Kareem Abdul-Jabbar ___ 17,440
5. Artis Gilmore _____ 16,330

REBOUNDS PER GAME
1. Wilt Chamberlain _____ 22.9
2. Bill Russell _____ 22.5
3. Bob Pettit _____ 16.2
4. Jerry Lucas _____ 15.6
5. Nate Thurmond _____ 15

ASSISTS
1. John Stockton _____ 15,806
2. Jason Kidd _____ 12,091
3. Steve Nash _____ 10,335
4. Mark Jackson _____ 10,334
5. Chris Paul* _____ 10,275

ASSISTS PER GAME
1. Magic Johnson _____ 11.2
2. John Stockton _____ 10.5
3. Oscar Robertson _____ 9.5
4. Chris Paul* _____ 9.4
5. Isiah Thomas _____ 9.3

STEALS
1. John Stockton _____ 3,265
2. Jason Kidd _____ 2,684
3. Michael Jordan _____ 2,514
4. Gary Payton _____ 2,445
5. Chris Paul* _____ 2,332

STEALS PER GAME
1. Alvin Robertson _____ 2.71
2. Micheal Ray Richardson ___ 2.63
3. Roland "Fatty" Taylor _____ 2.40
4. Michael Jordan _____ 2.35
5. Mookie Blaylock _____ 2.33

BLOCKED SHOTS
1. Hakeem Olajuwon _____ 3,830
2. Dikembe Mutombo _____ 3,289
3. Kareem Abdul-Jabbar ___ 3,189
4. Artis Gilmore _____ 3,178
5. Mark Eaton _____ 3,064

BLOCKED SHOTS PER GAME
1. Mark Eaton _____ 3.5
2. Manute Bol _____ 3.3
3. Hakeem Olajuwon _____ 3.1
4. David Robinson _____ 3
5. Elmore Smith _____ 2.9

TRIPLE-DOUBLES
1. Russell Westbrook* _____ 184
2. Oscar Robertson _____ 181
3. Magic Johnson _____ 138
4. Jason Kidd _____ 107
5. LeBron James* _____ 99

> * Indicates player is active as of 2021

GLOSSARY

assist

A pass from one teammate to another that directly leads to a basket.

conference

A group of sports teams, usually from a common region, who play against each other during the regular season.

double-double

Scoring at least ten points in two of five statistical categories.

draft

A process in which sports teams select the top eligible college and international players to join them.

draft lottery

An event that determines the order in which teams will select in the first round of the NBA Draft.

dynasty

An extended period of excellence or success for a team.

endorsement

An agreement where a business pays someone to recommend a product to the public.

field goal

A two- or three-point basket scored on any shot other than a free throw.

lane

Located on each end of a basketball court, the lane is the rectangular area close to the basket.

merge

To combine or unite into one.

rebound

A missed shot that is picked up by a player.

triple-double

Scoring at least ten points in three of five statistical categories.

veteran

An athlete who has played many years in the league.

TO LEARN MORE

FURTHER READINGS

Graves, Will. *NBA*. Abdo, 2021.

Gurnett, Bob. *LeBron James: G.O.A.T.* Sterling, 2019.

Mason, Tyler. *Ultimate NBA Road Trip*. Abdo, 2019.

ONLINE RESOURCES

To learn more about the NBA, please visit **abdobooklinks.com** or scan this QR code. These links are routinely monitored and updated to provide the most current information available.

INDEX

Cover Photos: Doug Duran/MediaNews Group/Bay Area News/Getty Images, front (Stephen Curry); Peter Southwick/AP Images, front (Larry Bird); Al Messerschmidt/AP Images, front (Michael Jordan); David Zalubowski/AP Images, front (Kevin Durant); Focus on Sport/Getty Images, front (Earvin Magic Johnson), back (Kareem Abdul-Jabbar); Ezra Shaw/Getty Images Sport/Getty Images, front (LeBron James); Wally Skalij/Los Angeles Times/Getty Images, front (Kobe Bryant); Jonathan Daniel/Getty Images Sport/Getty Images, back (Giannis Antetokounmpo)

Interior Photos: Matt Patterson/AP Images, 1; Lachlan Cunningham/Getty Images Sport/Getty Images, 3, 24–25; John W. McDonough/Sports Illustrated/Getty Images, 4; Bettmann/Getty Images, 5; Frank Franklin II/AP Images, 6; Charles Knoblock/AP Images, 8, 170 (top); Brian Rothmuller/Icon Sportswire/AP Images, 10; AP Images, 12, 15, 31, 32–33, 81, 111, 118, 130, 131, 134, 147, 154 (bottom), 161 (bottom), 168 (top), 169, 177 (bottom), 178; Sam Myers/AP Images, 13; Bill Chaplis/AP Images, 14; Richard Mackson/Sports Illustrated/Getty Images, 17; David Scarbrough/AP Images, 18–19; Eric Gay/AP Images, 20, 26–27, 69, 133, 181; Tony Dejak/AP Images, 21; J. Pat Carter/AP Images, 22–23; Curtis Compton/Atlanta Journal-Constitution/AP Images, 28; Charles Kelly/AP Images, 30, 182; Mary Schwalm/AP Images, 34–35; F. Carter Smith/AP Images, 35; Kathy Willens/AP Images, 37, 106–107, 158; Focus on Sport/Getty Images, 38, 148, 157 (right), 162 (top); Lennox McLendon/AP Images, 39, 59, 160; Nick Wass/AP Images, 40, 48–49, 145; Nell Redmond/AP Images, 41; Chuck Burton/AP Images, 42; Ron Frehm/AP Images, 43, 75; Nam Y. Huh/AP Images, 44; David Banks/AP Images, 45; John Swart/AP Images, 47, 165; Beck Diefenbach/AFP/Getty Images, 50–51; Al Behrman/AP Images, 51; Ashley Landis/AP Images, 52; David J. Phillip/AP Images, 54; Tom DiPace/AP Images, 55; David Zalubowski/AP Images, 56–57; Gary Stewart/AP Images, 58; Chase Stevens/AP Images, 60; Jennings/AP Images, 61; Duane Burleson/AP Images, 62; Elisa Amendola/AP Images, 63; Warren M. Winterbottom/AP Images, 64; Gloria Ferniz/AP Images, 65; Jeff Chiu/AP Images, 66–67, 96; Mark Mulligan/Houston Chronicle/AP Images, 68; Rick Bowmer/AP Images, 70, 71; Darron Cummings/AP Images, 72; George Gojkovich/Getty Images Sport/Getty Images, 74; Mark J. Terrill/AP Images, 76, 79, 80–81, 83, 90–91, 140–141; Chris Carlson/AP Images, 78; Brandon Bill/AP Images, 85; Ann Heisenfelt/AP Images, 86, 99; Matt Slocum/AP Images, 87, 103, 112, 144; John Raoux/AP Images, 88, 102, 163 (right); Alan Diaz/AP Images, 89, 174 (top); Wilfredo Lee/AP Images, 91; Paul Sancya/AP Images, 92–93, 150; Paul Shane/AP Images, 94; Fred Jewell/AP Images, 95; Bruce Kluckhohn/AP Images, 97; Kevin Reece/AP Images, 98; Ronald Cortes/Getty Images Sport/Getty Images, 101; Wendell Cruz/AP Images, 104; Dave Pickoff/AP Images, 107, 159 (bottom); Garett Fisbeck/AP Images, 108–109; Thearon W. Henderson/AP Images, 110; Steve Simoneau/AP Images, 113; Nathaniel S. Butler/NBAE/National Basketball Association/Getty Images, 115; John Bazemore/AP Images, 116–117; John W. McDonough/Icon Sportswire/AP Images, 119; Matt York/AP Images, 120, 128–129; RBK/AP Images, 122; Charles Bennett/AP Images, 123; Scott Troyanos/AP Images, 124; Craig Mitchelldyer/AP Images, 125; JV/AP Images, 127; Charles Krupa/AP Images, 135; Tannis Toohey/AP Images, 136; Frank Gunn/AP Images, 137, 138; Ben Margot/AP Images, 139; Tom Olmscheid/AP Images, 142; Jack Smith/AP Images, 143; NBA Photo Library/NBAE/National Basketball Association/Getty Images, 146; Winslow Townson/AP Images, 149; Roberto Borea/AP Images, 150–151; Rusty Kennedy/AP Images, 151; Harry Harris/AP Images, 152; Dick Raphael/NBAE/National Basketball Association/Getty Images, 153 (left), 180 (top); Rich Schultz/AP Images, 153 (right); Paul Vathis/AP Images, 154 (top); Marcio Jose Sanchez/AP Images, 155; Tony Guttierez/AP Images, 156; Alonzo Adams/AP Images, 157 (left); Bill Janscha/AP Images, 159 (top); Carlos Osorio/AP Images, 161 (top); Bill Kostroun/AP Images, 163 (left), 170 (bottom); Kevork Djansezian/AP Images, 164; Mark Humphrey/AP Images, 166 (top); Ross D. Franklin/AP Images, 166 (bottom); Bob Galbraith/AP Images, 167, 183; lodriguss/AP Images, 168 (bottom); Erik S. Lesser/AP Images, 171; Sue Ogrocki/AP Images, 172–173; Tim Johnson/AP Images, 173; Patrick Semansky/AP Images, 174 (bottom); NBA Photos/NBAE/National Basketball Association/Getty Images, 175; Jim Mone/AP Images, 176; Al Messerschmidt/AP Images, 177 (top); Jeff Haynes/AFP/Getty Images, 179 (left); Rick Stewart/Getty Images Sport Classic/Getty Images, 179 (right); Wen Roberts/NBAE/NBA Classic/Getty Images, 180 (bottom); Debby Wong/Shutterstock Images, 186; Matt Brown/iStockphoto, 187

ABDOBOOKS.COM

Published by Abdo Publishing, a division of ABDO, PO Box 398166, Minneapolis, Minnesota 55439. Copyright © 2022 by Abdo Consulting Group, Inc. International copyrights reserved in all countries. No part of this book may be reproduced in any form without written permission from the publisher. Abdo Reference™ is a trademark and logo of Abdo Publishing.

Printed in the United States of America, North Mankato, Minnesota.
062022
082022

Editor: Alyssa Sorenson
Series Designer: Colleen McLaren

LIBRARY OF CONGRESS CONTROL NUMBER: 2021941792

PUBLISHER'S CATALOGING-IN-PUBLICATION DATA
Names: Flynn, Brendan, author.
Title: The NBA encyclopedia for kids / by Brendan Flynn
Description: Minneapolis, Minnesota : Abdo Publishing, 2022 | Series: Sports encyclopedias for kids | Includes online resources and index.
Identifiers: ISBN 9781532196911 (lib. bdg.) | ISBN 9781532159992 (pbk.) | ISBN 9781098218720 (ebook)
Subjects: LCSH: Basketball--Juvenile literature. | Basketball teams--Juvenile literature. | Basketball players--Juvenile literature. | Basketball--Records--United States--Juvenile literature. | Professional sports--Juvenile literature.
Classification: DDC 796.32364097--dc23